CLEAN BREAK

presents

T0352661

HOUSE by Somalia Seaton

+

AMONGST THE REEDS
by Chino Odimba

House + Amongst the Reeds were first performed at
Assembly, George Square Theatre, The Box, Edinburgh,
on 4 August 2016

Before transferring to The Yard Theatre, London,
1 September 2016

HOUSE by Somalia Seaton

+

AMONGST THE REEDS
by Chino Odimba

CAST

HOUSE

Patricia	**Shvorne Marks**
Mama	**Michelle Greenidge**
Jemima	**Rebecca Omogbehin**

AMONGST THE REEDS

Oni	**Rebecca Omogbehin**
Gillian	**Jan Le**

CREATIVE TEAM

DIRECTOR	**Róisín McBrinn**
DESIGNER	**Rachael Canning**
LIGHTING DESIGNER	**Natasha Chivers**
SOUND DESIGNER	**Becky Smith**
ASSISTANT DIRECTOR	**Michal Keyamo**

Clean Break would like to acknowledge the generous support of all its funders and supporters with special thanks to Arts Council England, The Esmée Fairbairn Foundation and John Ellerman Foundation for supporting this double bill.

John Ellerman
Foundation

Introduction

House and *Amongst the Reeds* came out of an intense six-month Emerging Writers' Programme that we set up at Clean Break in September 2014. The scheme was set up, with the valuable support of the Manchester Royal Exchange, Tricycle Theatre and Bristol Old Vic, as an extension of our commitment to artist development and, specifically, to focus on diversifying the voices and insights that we bring to the stage. In our search for writers to work with, we made the focus about writers from Black, Asian and Minority Ethnic backgrounds, whose writing we loved, who have unique voices and who could thrive with time and expertise to focus on their craft and, most importantly, who would benefit hugely from having their work produced.

Our commitment to diversity is at the core of our work; the focus on voices from BAME women is particularly important given the over-representation of BAME people in prison – currently 26% of the prison population compared to 14% of the general population.

After six months of workshops, conversations with former Clean Break writers (thank you Chloë Moss, and Rebecca Prichard!) and learning about the work of Clean Break, each writer brought a question to the group specific to women who have been criminalised or who have experience of the criminal justice system. From there, we created opportunities relating to the writers' areas of interest. Somalia taught playwriting with me on our London Theatre Education Programme, and delivered a writing residency in prison, as well as discussing the issues around oppression and denial of mental health, that were amongst the starting points for her play, with our student support team. Chino made inroads close to her home in Bristol with a Refugee and Asylum Seekers group, as well as speaking to legal professionals about the criminalisation of women who are without legal status in this country. She also taught on our Education Programme and with young people who had asylum applications pending.

And then gradually, the plays started to appear. We are delighted to be producing these two brave voices and we look forward to being part of their artistic growth into the future. Thank you to all the organisation and individuals who have support Clean Break's Emerging Writers' Scheme.

Róisín McBrinn
Director, *House + Amongst the Reeds*
Head of Artistic Programme, Clean Break

Cast and Creative Team

Chino Odimba (writer)
Chino has been on attachment to Clean Break through its Emerging Writers' Programme since 2014. Credits include: *A Blues for Nia* (Eclipse Theatre/BBC); *His name is Ishmael* (Bristol Old Vic, 2013); *The Birdwoman of Lewisham* (Arcola, 2015); and *Joanne* for Clean Break (Soho Theatre, 2015). Chino is a winner of the Channel 4 Playwrights' Scheme 2016 (formerly the Pearson Playwrights' Scheme) and is on attachment with Talawa Theatre Company.

Somalia Seaton (writer)
Somalia has been on attachment to Clean Break through its Emerging Writers' Programme since 2014. She trained at East 15 Acting School and is Artistic Director of No Ball Games Allowed, creating work with young people at its core. Her debut play *Crowning Glory* (Theatre Royal Stratford East) was shortlisted for the 2014 Alfred Fagon Award, and her play *Fall of the Kingdom, Rise of the Foot Soldier* is produced at the RSC (2016). She recently completed a commission from The Yard Theatre, and her commissions to Talawa and The Bush, which she received while on the Talawa Writers' Programme, are currently in development. She is now under commission to the National Youth Theatre.

Shvorne Marks (Patricia)
Theatre credits include: *The Brink*, *Macbeth* (Orange Tree, Richmond); *Flare Path* (UK tour); *The Witch of Edmonton* (RSC); *The Tea Party* (Park); *Some Other Mother* (Traverse); *Home* (The Last Refuge); *Trust Fund* (Bush); *Seasoned* (Tobacco Factory). TV includes *Endeavour* (series II and III) and *Holby City*. Audio includes: *Doctor Who* (BBC); *DNA* (Listening Books); and *Bridge to the Wounded Heart* (Gap Digital).

Rebecca Omogbehin (Jemima and Oni)
Rebecca trained at Mountview Academy of Theatre Arts. Recent credits include: *Soho Young Playwrights Project* (Soho); *Casualty* (BBC); *How Nigeria Became*, *Seesaw* (Unicorn); *Crowning Glory* (Theatre Royal Stratford East); *Oil City* (Platform for the Arts Admin Festival); *Snow Ghost's Murder Cries* (Music Video, Epoch Films).

Jan Le (Gillian)
Jan Le began her training at a young age with the Young Actors Theatre. After a brief break from performing in order to complete her degree in Politics and International Relations, she has returned to theatre and is delighted to be making her professional debut in *Amongst the Reeds*.

Michelle Greenidge (Mama)
Michelle Greenidge trained as an actor at Morley College. Last year she featured in the Sky Drama *Venus Vs Mars,* and as Aunty Jeanie in the comedy series *All About the McKenzies*. This year is her big-screen debut in British feature film *The Intent* (2016). Film credits include: *Perceptions* and *Free*. Michelle played the part of Trissia, to great acclaim, in Nicola Baldwin's *All Saints*. She has appeared on stage at Theatre Royal Stratford East, working with Team Angelica and its director Rikki Beadle-

Blair MBE. Theatre credits include: *At the Feet of Jesus*, *Red Room*, *Super Skinny Bitches*, *England is De Place for Me*, *Omega Time*. Short films include: the award-winning *Leave* with Alexis Rodney, with Richie Campbell in *Sorry We Don't Help Darkies*, and alongside Rupert Fraser in *Crude*, *Class 15*, *Red Room*, *Daddy's Girl*, *The Day I Met My Mother*.

Róisín McBrinn (director)

Róisín is Head of Artistic Programme at Clean Break. Her first production for Clean Break was 2015's critically acclaimed *Joanne* (Soho, 2015 and RSC, Making Mischief festival 2016). She has directed productions for some of the UK and Ireland's most important theatres including: *Afterplay* by Brian Friel (Sheffield Crucible); *Yerma* by Lorca in a version by Ursula Rani Sarma (West Yorkshire Playhouse); *No Escape* by Mary Raftery, *Perve* by Stacey Gregg and *Heartbreak House* by GB Shaw (Abbey, Dublin); *66 Books* (Bush). She has developed new plays for the Traverse, the Bush, the National Theatre, Soho, the Abbey and the Royal Exchange, Manchester. She was Associate Director at Sherman Cymru until 2013, credits include: *Before It Rains* by Kath Chandler (co-production with Bristol Old Vic); *The Sleeping Beauties* and *Peter Pan* by Robert Alan Evans, *The Get Together* and *It's a Family Affair* by Simon Crowther, as well as leading the nurturing and development of Welsh and Wales-based new writing for the company. Róisín was the inaugural recipient of the Quercus Award 2010 run by the National Theatre and was resident at the National Theatre Studio in 2009. In 2004 she won the Young Vic/Jerwood Young Director's Award.

Rachael Canning (designer)

Rachael trained at the Royal Welsh College of Music and Drama and since then has worked as a set, costume and puppet designer. Rachael is co-director of The Wrong Crowd. Set and costume designs include: *Kite*, *Hag*, *The Girl with the Iron Claws* (The Wrong Crowd); *Swanhunter* (Opera North and The Wrong Crowd Co-production); *Magical Night* (Royal Opera House); *A Christmas Carol*, *Rapunzel* (Citizens, Glasgow) *Vernon God Little* (associate costume, Young Vic); *Porn the Musical* (Theatre503); *Mad Forest* (BAC); *Hansel and Gretel*, *Beauty and the Beast*, *Sleeping Beauties*, *The Snow Tiger* (Sherman Cymru); *The Tailor's Daughter* (WNO); *Peter Grimes* (Costume, Grand Theatre Geneva); *A Midsummer Night's Dream* (Regent's Park Open Air); *Fiddler on the Roof* (Aberystwyth Arts); *Purcell His Ground* (ENO). Puppet design and direction includes: *Into the Woods*, *The Jungle Book*, *Of Mice and Men* (West Yorkshire Playhouse); *The City Madam* (RSC); *The Firebird* (Dundee Rep); *The Three Musketeers and the Princess of Spain* (ETT/Traverse/Belgrade Theatre); *Into the Woods*, *Peter Pan* (Regent's Park Open Air/Public Theater, New York); *The Red Balloon* (Royal Opera House); *Sleeping Beauty* (Birmingham Rep); *Kes* (Sheffield Crucible); *Adrian Mole Aged 13¾* (Leicester Curve).

Natasha Chivers (lighting designer)

Natasha Chivers' work includes: *Sunset at the Villa Thalia* (National Theatre); *Strapless*, *Electric Counterpoint* (ROH); *Gravity Fatigue*, *Encore* (Sadler's Wells); *Oresteia* (Almeida/West End; 2016 Olivier nomination for Best Lighting); *1984* (Almeida, West End and tour); *That Face* (also West End), *Who Cares, Fireworks, Adler & Gibb, The Mistress Contract, Gastronauts, The Djinns of Eidgah* (Royal Court); *The Insatiable Inflatable Candylion, Mother Courage and her Children, The Radicalisation of Bradley Manning* (National Theatre Wales); *Praxis Makes Perfect* (Neon Neon/National Theatre Wales; Theatre Critics of Wales Award for Best Lighting); *Macbeth* (also Broadway and tour of Japan), *27, The Wheel, Mary Stuart, The House of Bernard Alba, Home* (National Theatre of Scotland); *Green Snake* (National Theatre of China); *Statement of Regret* (National Theatre); *Sunday in the Park with George* (West End; Olivier Award for Best Lighting Design); *The Wolves in the Walls* (National Theatre of Scotland/Improbable); *Othello, Dirty Wonderland, pool (no water), Tiny Dynamite, Peepshow, Hymns , Sell-Out* (Frantic Assembly); *Four Fridas, Run!, Renaissance* (Greenwich + Docklands International Festivals); *Mesmerics, Metheus* (BalletBoyz The Talent/Linbury Studio); *Motor Show* (LIFT and the Brighton Festival); *Electric Hotel* (Sadler's Wells/Fuel); *God's Garden* (Arthur Pita at ROH Linbury and tour); *Broken, Scattered* (Motionhouse). Natasha also won a Theatre Award UK for Best Design (with Lizzie Clachan) in 2011 for *Happy Days* (Sheffield Crucible).

Becky Smith (sound designer)
Becky studied drama at Exeter University. Her sound designs for Clean Break include: *Joanne* (Soho and The Other Place, RSC); *Little on the inside* (Summerhall, Edinburgh); *Billy the Girl* (Soho): *it felt empty…* (Arcola); *A Just Act* (prison tour); *This Wide Night* (Soho); *Missing Out* (prison tour). Other sound designs include: *36 Phonecalls* (Hampstead Downstairs); *The Day After* (VAULT Festival); *Bird* (Derby Playhouse); *Circles, Frozen* (Birmingham Rep); *The Only Way is Chelsea's* (York Theatre Royal); *The Kitchen Sink* (Hull Truck); *The Well and the Badly Loved, Lagan* (Ovalhouse); *Cardboard Dad* (Sherman Cymru); *Brood* (Theatre Royal Stratford East); *The Juniper Tree* (UK tour); *Reverence* (Southwark Playhouse); *The Ghost Sonata* (Trinity Buoy Wharf). Becky also freelances in Radio Drama for the BBC.

Michal Keyamo (assistant director)
Since graduating as a Bachelor of Law in 2013, Michal Keyamo has focused on work as a director, performer and facilitator. She has previously worked as an assistant director as Blue/Orange with Matthew Xia at the Young Vic (part of the Young Vic's Jerwood Assistant Director Programme 2016, supported by the Jerwood Charitable Foundation). Other assisting and directing credits include: Boris Karloff Trainee Assistant Director, *Macbeth*, Carrie Cracknell (Young Vic); Director, *Mine* (New Heritage Theatre and Paddington Arts Centre); Director, *10-10-10 Festival* (Intermission Thjeatre). Credits as a performer include: *King Lear* (Globe to Globe at Shakespeare's Globe); *Handa's Surprise* (Little Angel); *Red Forest* (Belarus Free Theatre at the Young Vic).

Ali Beale (production manager)
Ali has worked in theatre, opera, film, dance, performance and installation, including both national and international tours. She is also production manager and co-designer for Fevered Sleep. Recent work includes: *The Taming of the Shrew* (Shakespeare's Globe); *Who Cares, Plaques and Tangles, You for Me for You* (Royal Court); *Pests, Billy the Girl, Re-Charged, A Just Act, it felt empty..., Missing Out, This Wide Night, Black Crows* (Clean Break); *Men and Girls Dance, Dusk, Above Me the Wide Blue Sky, Little Universe, It's the Skin You're Living In, Still Life with Dog, The Weather Factory, On Ageing, The Bounce, The Forest, Brilliant, Stilled, An Infinite Line Brighton, And the Rain Falls Down, The Summer Subversive, Fleet, The Field of Miracles, Feast Your Eyes* (Fevered Sleep); *The Contents of a House, Guided Tour* (Peter Reder; touring to Gijon, Pittsburgh, Arizona, Singapore, Bucharest and Moscow); *Kingdom of Earth* (Three-Legged Theatre); *The Kingdom* (The Print Room); *Under Glass, Must, Performing Medicine, Sampled, Fantastic Voyage* (The Clod Ensemble); *The Evocation of Papa Mas, The Firework Maker's Daughter, Aladdin, Playing the Victim, A Little Fantasy, Shoot Me in the Heart* (Told by An Idiot); *Gumbo Jumbo* (The Gogmagogs); *The Ratcatcher of Hamlin* (Cartoon De Salvo); *Oogly Boogly* (Tom Morris and Guy Dartnel); *Throat* (Company FZ); *Arcane* (Opera Circus).

Roisin Symes (company stage manager)
Roisin trained on the Stage Management and Technical Theatre Course at LAMDA. Theatre credits include: *After Independence* (Arcola); *The Bear* (Polka/Albany Deptford); *Love Birds: The Musical* (Pleasance Edinburgh); *Unearthed* (UK tour); *Donkey Heart* (Trafalgar Studios/Old Red Lion); *Eye of a Needle* (Southwark Playhouse); *Coolatully, Unscorched, Pack, Rigor Mortis* (Finborough); *Superior Donuts* (Southwark Playhouse); *The Matchgirls* (Wilton's Music Hall); *The Magpies, the Wolves* (Tristan Bates); *Orlando* (Battersea Arts Centre); *Many Moons* (Theatre503).

Anna Sheard (deputy stage manager)
Anna trained in Stage Management and Technical Theatre at the Royal Welsh College of Music and Drama. Her credits include: *10,000 Smarties* (Arts at the Old Fire Station, Oxford); *The Buskers Opera* (Park); *The Importance of Being Earnest* (ROH, Barbican); stage manager (Urdang Academy 2014 and 2016); *Aladdin* and *Danny the Champion of the World* (London Contemporary Theatre UK tour); *Alice's Adventures in Wonderland* (Opera Holland Park); *Medea* (Gate); *Sweet Charity* (NYMT); *Farragut North* (Southwark Playhouse); *Lotty's War* (UK tour); *Dancing at Lughnasa* (Theatre by the Lake); *Spamalot* (ATG); *Lizzie Siddal* (Arcola); *An Incident at the Border* (Finborough/Trafalgar Studios).

Beverley Richards (trainee assistant stage manager)
A current Clean Break student, Beverley has held a fervent ambition to work in professional theatre production ever since studying theatre at City Lit several years ago. This is her debut professional production, and she is determined that it will be the first of many.

For *House + Amongst the Reeds*

Production Team
Senior Producer **Helen Pringle**
Producer **Emma Waslin**
Production Manager **Ali Beale**
Company Stage Manager **Roisin Symes**
Deputy Stage Manager **Anna Sheard**
Trainee Assistant Stage Manager **Beverley Richards**

Marketing and Press
Marketing Consultants **The Cogency**
Press Consultant **Nancy Poole PR**

Clean Break Executive Director Lucy Perman MBE
Clean Break Marketing Assistant Caroline Boss

Thanks

The company would like to thank Dr Judith Gurry, Sharon
Duncan Brewster, Raike Ayola, Vivienne Acheampong,
Vera Chok, Ruth Chingwada-Bailey, Suzanne Bell, Sonali
Naik, Jaqueline Stewart, Sharon Clarke, Nic Wass, Lolo
Hughes, The National Theatre Studio, The Tricycle
Theatre, Bristol Old Vic, and Manchester Royal
Exchange.

Special thanks go to Jane Fallowfield and Emteaz
Hussain.

For Clean Break

Executive Director   **Lucy Perman MBE**
Head of Finance and Senior Producer   **Helen Pringle**
Head of Artistic Programme   **Róisín McBrinn**
Head of Education   **Anna Herrmann**
Head of Engagement   **Imogen Ashby**
Assistant Head of Education (Learning)   **Vishni Velada-Billson**
Assistant Head of Education (Student Services)   **Jacqueline Stewart**
Interim General Manager   **CJ Dyson**
Producer   **Emma Waslin**
Theatre Education Manager   **Laura McCluskey**
Theatre Education Manager   **Lorraine Faissal**
Student Support Worker   **Grace Adejuwon**
Student Support Worker   **Carole Jarvis**
Outreach Worker   **Lauren Sammé**
Digital Artist in Residence   **Natasha McDonnell**
Volunteer Coordinator   **Samantha McNeil**
Senior Development Manager   **Lillian Ashford**
Development Manager   **Emily Goodyer**
Development Adviser   **Liz Banner**
Marketing Assistant   **Caroline Boss**
Executive Assistant   **Lauren Mooney**
Interim Finance Manager   **Annette Bennett**
Finance Administrator   **Selina Mayer**
Office Administrator   **Lucy Grant**
Administrative Assistant   **Jeanette Robinson**
Education Administrator   **Verity LaRoche**
Cleaner   **Pauline Bernard**

Board of Directors
Kim Evans OBE (Chair), Suzanne Bell, Jude Boyles, Deborah Coles, Doreen Foster, Lucy Kirkwood, Alice Millest, Sonali Naik, Susan J Royce, Tanya Tracey, Despina Tsatsas, Denise White

Patrons
Lord Paul Boateng, Carmen Callil, Dame Judi Dench DBE, Sir Richard Eyre CBE, Barbara Hosking CBE, Baroness Helena Kennedy QC, Kevin McGrath OBE DL, Ann Mitchell, Yve Newbold LLB, Baroness Usha Prashar CBE, Dr Joan Scanlon JP, Baroness Vivien Stern CBE, Dame Janet Suzman DBE, Emma Thompson, Dame Harriet Walter DBE, Lia Williams

Clean Break
2 Patshull Road
London
NW5 2LB
Registered company number 2690758
Registered charity number 1017560

Tel: 020 7482 8600
Fax: 020 7482 8611
general@cleanbreak.org.uk
www.cleanbreak.org.uk
facebook.com/cleanbreak
@CleanBrk

Clean Break would like to acknowledge the generous support of all its funders and supporters. Clean Break is a member of ITC.

CLEAN BREAK

Acclaimed theatre company Clean Break produces ground-breaking plays with women writers and actors at the heart of its work. Founded in 1979 by two women prisoners who needed urgently to tell their stories through theatre, the company today has an independent education programme delivering theatre opportunities to women offenders and women at risk, in custodial and community settings. Clean Break's innovative education work, combined with visionary expertise in theatre, makes for a powerful mix. Celebrated by critics and audience across the UK, the company's award winning plays hit a collective nerve, humanising some of the most difficult things we need to talk about as a society.

Recent productions include: *Joanne* (Soho Theatre and The Other Place, RSC); Vivienne Franzmann's *Pests* (Royal Exchange Theatre /Royal Court Theatre co-production and touring); Katie Hims' *Billy the Girl* (Soho Theatre and prison tour); Suhayla El-Bushra's *Fingertips* (Latitude); Alice Birch's *Little on the inside* (Almeida, Latitude and Edinburgh); Rebecca Prichard's *Dream Pill* (Almeida, Edinburgh and touring); *There Are Mountains* by Chloë Moss (HMP & YOI Askham Grange); *Re-Charged* (Soho Theatre London 2011); *Charged* (Soho Theatre 2010); *it felt empty when the heart went at first but it is alright now* by Lucy Kirkwood (Arcola Theatre, joint winner of the John Whiting Award 2010); and *This Wide Night* by Chloë Moss (Soho Theatre 2008 and revived in 2009, winner of the Susan Smith Blackburn Award 2009).

Productions from Graduates of our Theatre Education Programme include: *Spent* by Katherine Chandler (tour); *Sweatbox* by Chloë Moss (Latitude and tour); *Meal Ticket* devised in collaboration with Forced Entertainment (Latitude); *Frientimacy* by Stacey Gregg (Donmar Studios); *Sounds Like An Insult* by Vivienne Franzmann; *This is Where We're From* by Morgan Lloyd Malcolm (Clean Break Studios); *Stepping Off the Edge of the World* by Roz Wyllie (tour); and *Hours til' Midnight* by Sonya Hale (tour).

Changing lives and changing minds appeal – help us make a difference

'I've seen the impact of Clean Break's work – both on the women it works with in prisons and students on its London education programme, and on audiences in theatres across the country. It is an organisation that changes lives and changes minds.'
Dame Harriet Walter DBE, Actor and Clean Break Patron

Most of the 3,900 women in prison each year are serving sentences for non-violent crime, often linked to poor mental health, addiction, poverty, racism and lack of education. The majority are themselves victims of crime and due to their frequent caring responsibilities and high support needs, their offending has a disproportionate social and economic impact. Empowering these women to overcome the often significant challenges they face can therefore transform not only their lives but our society.

There is no other organisation like Clean Break in the UK. For 37 years we have continuously made a difference to the lives of women offenders (from age 17) and today, we are widely recognised as a sector leader in criminal justice, women's development and the cultural industries.

Your support will help Clean Break make a difference:

- engaging audiences and creating debate through bold new plays by the UK's most exciting women playwrights addressing the theme of women, crime and justice;
- building confidence, skills and qualifications for women in prison, former offenders and women at risk of offending;
- professional development for criminal justice staff, using short productions, training and discussion to deepen understanding and reconnect professionals with women's experiences.

As a registered charity, our work is only possible thanks to support from individuals and organisations who share our commitment to transforming the lives of vulnerable women affected by the criminal justice system. Donations can be made by sending a cheque by post, online at www.cleanbreak.org.uk or by texting 'CBT02' followed by your chosen amount (for example 'CBT02 £10') to 70070. Every donation can make a lasting difference. If you would like to find out more about supporting Clean Break, please contact Elizabeth Banner, Development Adviser on 020 7482 8608 or liz.banner@cleanbreak.org.uk.

Thank you for your support.

HOUSE

Somalia Seaton

Characters

PATRICIA, *mid- to late thirties*
JEMIMA, *late twenties*
MAMA, *fifties*

Note on Text

/ indicates the point at which the next speaker interrupts

This text went to press before the end of rehearsals and so may differ slightly from the play as performed

Scene One

We hear female voices singing, we don't know where they are yet.

Each of them in a different space and time.

Room is dark.

Voices sing.

In tandem.

VOICES   Glory glory glory!
You are my
glory glory glory. You are my father father father,
you fill me with
Your mighty mighty spirit,
I am, forever thankful for your love,
you lift me high, glory glory glory,
I'm thankful for
Your power and your mercy,
I'll never forget you heavenly father,
I am not worthy of your mercy...

JEMIMA *arrives in her living room. She is unsettled, she attempts to tidy. She sits. She stands. She fusses.*

The song continues.

PATRICIA *approaches the microphone. She drags it under the table with her, making sure no one has seen where she hides.*

As she does, we hear a WOMAN*'s voice in prayer, almost inaudible, the voice speaks in tongues underneath* PATRICIA*'s voice.*

All else is in darkness.

PATRICIA   It's me.

Hey little one.

Didn't get much sleep last night. You wouldn't
settle down. Put you on my chest not once but
maybe twice. They say skin to skin is the best, but
I did that, not once but maybe twice. No joy.

Last night, in between tears and midnight screams
I forgot how much my heart sings when I hear you
breathe.

How the smell of your breath makes the hairs on
the back of my neck stand tall with ease, how if I
listen really carefully, I hear your name in every
melody.

I wanna scoop you up and spin you round, top you
up with love till you overflow, place you on a star
and watch you glide through our galaxy.

Because you deserve, the stars, and the moon and
all in between, you deserve the world little one,
I'll give you the stars and the moon and all in
between. You are my moon and my stars and all in
between, the banoffee to my pie.

(*Laughs*.) Apple of my eye… Am I embarrassing
you?

Am I?

Good!

A different space.

Lights up on MAMA.

MAMA   (*Sings*.) Glory glory glory!
You are my
Glory glory glory. You are my father father father,
you fill me with
Your mighty mighty spirit,
I am, forever thankful for your love,
You lift me high, glory glory glory,

                I'm thankful for
                Your power and your mercy,
                I'll never forget you heavenly father,
                I am not worthy of your mercy...

PATRICIA   Little one. Little one come on little one wake up,
                back on my chest little one. Come back. Come on.
                Come back little one.

                Lights down on PATRICIA.

                MAMA*'s singing continues.*

Scene Two

MAMA*'s house.*

An open-plan kitchen/living room. Perfectly chaotic. It is reminiscent of 'immigrant done good'. Plastic on chairs, plastic tablecloths, endless stacks of papers and books, mismatched ornaments, un-hung family pictures, the coffee table has receipts and newspapers and crocheted mats. Jesus is here too, in every corner we are reminded of His face. A large framed portrait of Him hangs over the dining table.

JEMIMA   I wasn't sure if you'd come...

PATRICIA   ...Seems brighter somehow, like...

JEMIMA   But you're here...

PATRICIA   Like.

JEMIMA   You look...

PATRICIA   ...The sun has chosen this house out of all the
                houses...

JEMIMA   You look well...

PATRICIA   ...Like it had never chosen this house before...

JEMIMA   ...I mean good, you look good.

PATRICIA   … Almost like the outside has been allowed in…

JEMIMA   I wasn't sure…

PATRICIA   … like it's been invited in…

JEMIMA   When I didn't hear back…

PATRICIA   … A day blessed by light… a sign even…

JEMIMA   I guess I assumed, shouldn't have assumed. Sorry, I'm talking a lot I am, I'm talking a lot. Would you like to sit?

Beat.

MAMA *stops singing.*

They arrive into the same room.

PATRICIA *doesn't move.*

It's awkward for a moment.

PATRICIA   Bus was late.

JEMIMA   No problem.

PATRICIA   Traffic's nuts out there.

JEMIMA   Sales I bet.

PATRICIA   Work all year to buy Christmas gifts, broke as a joke, know you're broke! Yet you still hit them sales!

JEMIMA   One of those things I suppose.

PATRICIA   Shops must be ram.

JEMIMA   Probably.

PATRICIA   She's not back yet?

JEMIMA   Nah.

Beat.

PATRICIA   Bought flowers, left 'em on the bus.

JEMIMA   Don't worry about that.

PATRICIA   Tulips.

JEMIMA   Nice.

PATRICIA   Her favourite.

JEMIMA   That's right.

PATRICIA   Not no skinny bunch neither.

JEMIMA   I'd hope not!

PATRICIA   Told the lady to make 'em look pretty, told the
            lady they were Mum's favourite and it was her
            birthday so they best be pretty, then I go and
            bloody leave 'em on the bus.

JEMIMA   You're all the gift she needs.

PATRICIA   Some little shit'll have their mucky hands all over
            'em by now won't they?

            Sorry.

            Now who's talking too much?

JEMIMA   (*Smiles*.) Can I get you something?

PATRICIA   I'm good.

JEMIMA   A drink?

PATRICIA   Nah.

JEMIMA   Tea?

PATRICIA   Nah.

JEMIMA   Scotch?

            Beat.

PATRICIA   Not for me.

JEMIMA   Course, sorry.

PATRICIA   That's alright.

JEMIMA   Bad joke.

PATRICIA   It's all good sis.

JEMIMA   Right.

            Beat.

PATRICIA   Glad you called.

JEMIMA   Well I thought you might forget.

PATRICIA   Oh God, no.

JEMIMA   I mean, of course not just that…

PATRICIA   Marked it on my calender as soon as you left.

JEMIMA   Great.

PATRICIA   Yeah.

JEMIMA   I mean, it would have been fine if you had forgotten.

PATRICIA   I didn't forget.

JEMIMA   I just mean… it's January.

PATRICIA   I know what month it is.

JEMIMA   Of course Pat.

PATRICIA   *And* I'm fine.

JEMIMA   I know.

PATRICIA   Good.

JEMIMA   Just… when I didn't hear from you on Tuesday I thought you might…

PATRICIA   I took myself out for the day.

JEMIMA   That's nice.

PATRICIA   To mark it.

JEMIMA   I'm glad.

PATRICIA   Always mark it.

JEMIMA   I was worried.

PATRICIA   Needn't be.

JEMIMA   I just thought I'd try you on the off-chance you wanted to…

PATRICIA   I was fine.

JEMIMA   Just if you had wanted company to talk about… anything… I'd have sat with you.

PATRICIA   Wasn't necessary.

           Beat.

JEMIMA   I prayed for her… on Tuesday.

PATRICIA   Oh yeah?

JEMIMA   Don't usually go to that service, but needed to pray…

PATRICIA   Thanks.

JEMIMA   …felt like I should, do something.

PATRICIA   And it made you feel better?

JEMIMA   Useful.

PATRICIA   To who?

JEMIMA   To you I suppose.

PATRICIA   Cool.

           It's awkward.

           Beat.

JEMIMA   Oh, how was the move?

PATRICIA   Yeah…

JEMIMA   You never got back to me…

PATRICIA   It was all good in the end…

JEMIMA   You saw my call right?

PATRICIA   We'd finished.

JEMIMA   Sorry.

PATRICIA   All good.

JEMIMA   Work was…

PATRICIA   Literally, no problem…

JEMIMA   Seriously, if I could have…

PATRICIA   I know.

JEMIMA   Good.

PATRICIA   Busy woman!

JEMIMA   Could say that.

PATRICIA   Been busy myself actually…

JEMIMA   Yeah?

PATRICIA   …Interviews, decorating…

JEMIMA   Wicked…

PATRICIA   Carpet was rank so I had some friends help me pull it up.

JEMIMA   Oh, good.

PATRICIA   It'll do for now.

JEMIMA   So this place is nicer than your last one?

PATRICIA   I'd say so.

JEMIMA   They said you were in Catford.

PATRICIA   Back a Tescos.

JEMIMA   Bit grim round there.

PATRICIA   Nah not that bad.

JEMIMA   And the interviews?

PATRICIA   Yeah, really good. Decided I was gonna get my catering level two.

JEMIMA   Amazing!

PATRICIA   Yeah, study in the evenings, work during the day.

JEMIMA   That's really brilliant.

PATRICIA   Should be yeah.

JEMIMA   It will be.

PATRICIA   I think so, yeah… There's a few companies that were recommended, and yeah… interviews went well, so…

JEMIMA   That's / wicked Pat, so proud of you.

PATRICIA   Cheers.

Beat.

You / look…

JEMIMA   Some / water…

They laugh.

PATRICIA   Sorry, you / go.

JEMIMA   Sorry, no you.

PATRICIA   Ah I was just… You look well… You look beautiful.

JEMIMA   Don't feel it.

PATRICIA   So much to say, but then the words come out and they don't match.

JEMIMA   Do you want some water or…

PATRICIA   Honestly, I'm good.

Beat.

JEMIMA   You are?

PATRICIA   Already said that.

JEMIMA   Sorry, yeah…

PATRICIA   Still finding my feet.

JEMIMA   Course.

PATRICIA   I've got a lot of support, don't worry.

JEMIMA   Yeah…

PATRICIA   I'm focused…

JEMIMA   On?

PATRICIA   Living.

JEMIMA   Good.

PATRICIA   Stronger.

JEMIMA   Well that's great.

PATRICIA   Should could visit some time.

JEMIMA   I'd like that.

PATRICIA   Grab some food…

JEMIMA   Yeah, or…

PATRICIA   Cinema…

JEMIMA   Yeah…

PATRICIA   Something like that.

JEMIMA   Sure.

           You look…

PATRICIA   …like you saw me yesterday?

JEMIMA   (*Knowingly laughs.*) A little.

PATRICIA   Like no time has passed?

           I just stopped by to borrow a dress or something.

JEMIMA   Like we went out for dinner last night, woke up
           with a hangover and you've popped round to eat
           a kebab and watch Netflix on the sofa.

PATRICIA   Did I hold afresh first?

JEMIMA   Probably not.

PATRICIA   Brushed my teeth though yeah?

JEMIMA   Mmmmm, possible, but I'd say no. The
           hangover's nuts, best you could handle was
           throwing on some clothes and jumping in a cab!

PATRICIA   Not even a bus?

JEMIMA   Nah, today's not the one for dealing with random
             humans on no bus!

PATRICIA   True.

JEMIMA   Plus, the stench of last night's hopes and dreams
             vomited up on the top deck will only bring your
             breakfast up!

PATRICIA   Ha! People love vomiting on the night bus innit.

JEMIMA   It's rank.

PATRICIA   Never catch me vomiting on no bus.

JEMIMA   I'd *like* to be able to vomit.

PATRICIA   Why?!

JEMIMA   Never been able to.

PATRICIA   It's your mind protecting you, you fool! Count
             yaself lucky.

JEMIMA   You think?

PATRICIA   Our minds close off from the things we can't
             handle.

JEMIMA   I guess.

             You gonna take that off?

PATRICIA   I'm cold.

JEMIMA   Sorry I was airing the kitchen.

             Goes to close the window.

PATRICIA   Smells the same in here…

             Beat.

JEMIMA   Don't get me started!

PATRICIA   Like oil…

JEMIMA   Palm oil even!

PATRICIA   Yes! And plantain frying.

JEMIMA   Crayfish drying!

PATRICIA   Rice burning!

JEMIMA   Stew boiling!

PATRICIA   Katrina's mum.

JEMIMA   Ergh.

             And her burnt stew!

PATRICIA   Nasty!

JEMIMA   I saw her ya know.

PATRICIA   No way!

JEMIMA   Sends her regards.

PATRICIA   You sure 'bout that?

JEMIMA   Well, she said she hopes you're well.

PATRICIA   With her fake ass.

JEMIMA   She ain't that bad.

PATRICIA   If you say so.

JEMIMA   Got another baby on the way actually.

PATRICIA   Is it now?

JEMIMA   Eldest is five I think.

PATRICIA   But she ain't with the same guy is she?

JEMIMA   Nah.

PATRICIA   Not married neither, nah?

JEMIMA   Engaged.

PATRICIA   Yeah alright!

JEMIMA   Well, it's a commitment.

PATRICIA   Kinda.

JEMIMA   No it is, he didn't just get her pregnant and leave
             Pat.

PATRICIA   I suppose.

JEMIMA   She's tried her best.

PATRICIA   Well her best don't mean shit to the naysayers
             chatting her name and running their gums.

JEMIMA   You know people love to chat.

PATRICIA   I know her mother loves to chat.

JEMIMA   I guess.

PATRICIA   You guess? You forgotten she was the most vocal
             'bout my business.

JEMIMA   People grow init.

PATRICIA   Nah not them people, they grow more ignorant,
             get more set in their ways… Churchgoers, yet the
             first in line to persecute you.

JEMIMA   Not everyone Pat.

PATRICIA   All good though.

             Beat.

JEMIMA   Yeah, well. We live and learn.

PATRICIA   We do indeed.

JEMIMA   And you're doing great.

PATRICIA   I am.

JEMIMA   Exactly.

PATRICIA   Life's bless.

             PATRICIA *wanders around the room, stopping
             and taking it all in as she travels through.*
             JEMIMA *watches her silently.*

JEMIMA   Standing at the back of practice eating Haribos,
             when we should have been warming up our
             voices.

PATRICIA   (*Looks at her, confused.*) Err.

JEMIMA   Think.

PATRICIA   It's not coming.

JEMIMA   Eyes?

PATRICIA   Yes!

           Err… closing our eyes counting to five then running.

JEMIMA   Yes!

           First one to bump into the chair had to do a forfeit.

PATRICIA   I don't remember that.

JEMIMA   Carry on.

PATRICIA   Err singing like no one else in the world existed but us?

JEMIMA   Yes.

           Beat.

           I'd find you hiding round the side of your chest of drawers, headphones in, eyes closed just singing like nothing else in the whole world mattered, and you'd let me come hide there with you, hold ya hand, take out one of your headphones, stick it in my ear and just harmonise with you.

PATRICIA   You remember the weirdest of things I swear.

JEMIMA   Carry on.

PATRICIA   Nah, I'm good sis.

JEMIMA   Sing with me then.

PATRICIA   No!

JEMIMA   Come on!

PATRICIA   Are you alright?

JEMIMA   Seriously!

PATRICIA   What for?!

JEMIMA   Because we can.

PATRICIA   You're weird!

JEMIMA   I get it, why sing when you know you're always off-key.

PATRICIA   Excuse me?

JEMIMA   I'm just saying…

PATRICIA   What / exactly?

JEMIMA   … Some of us can sing and some of us cannot.

PATRICIA   Coming from Miss 'I used to stand in the back so no one notices you ain't singing along with the rest of us'.

JEMIMA   Don't act like you don't know 'bout my skills sis…

PATRICIA   What skills?!

JEMIMA   … cos we know when I start hitting those notes, it's gonna be nuts for your self-esteem!

PATRICIA   Hit which note? On what planet? Not this planet!

JEMIMA   (*Sings*.) Are you sure about alla that!?

            They burst into laughter.

PATRICIA   You're a mess sis!

JEMIMA   Alright.

            Beat.

PATRICIA   Let me see ya hand then!

            JEMIMA *holds out her hand with pride.*

JEMIMA   Told him I didn't want nothing fancy.

PATRICIA   I can tell.

JEMIMA   Oi!

PATRICIA   Well you two certainly didn't waste no time.

JEMIMA   I know.

PATRICIA   Well if you're sure?

JEMIMA   I am.

PATRICIA   Still punching above his weight though!

JEMIMA   I love being with him. I enjoy being with him.

PATRICIA   Bet he enjoys them breasts!

JEMIMA   Pat!

PATRICIA   Your tits have got flippin' massive!

JEMIMA   No they haven't!

PATRICIA   They're huge.

I can't stop staring at them.

JEMIMA   Smaller than yours.

PATRICIA   Massive fuckin' tits.

JEMIMA   Moving on!

PATRICIA   Don't tell me the word tits still embarrasses you.

JEMIMA   No actually, just…

PATRICIA   Prude.

JEMIMA   No I'm not.

PATRICIA   If you say so.

JEMIMA   What do you know anyway?

PATRICIA   That you need to liberate ya vagina before you sign your life away!

JEMIMA   Well I'm engaged so…

PATRICIA   But is he engaged with his dick game though?

JEMIMA   I'm not discussing my intimate time with you…

PATRICIA   Ain't one of those 'I don't do the nasty' type of church dudes is he…

JEMIMA   … We're not doing this…

PATRICIA   …Bible in the left hand whilst his right is up some
next woman's skirt?

JEMIMA   No…

PATRICIA   …Quoting the Bible whilst they sleep with every
piece of vagina floating past them, because your
last boyfriend looked like he didn't even know
how to spell cunnilingus…

JEMIMA   Patricia…

PATRICIA   …*Meanwhile* he was a proper gyalist…

JEMIMA   Yes alright…

PATRICIA   …A wolf in sheep's clothing if you will! Besides
a man that can't spell cunnilingus has no right
sniffin' round my sister's fanny…

JEMIMA   COULD YOU JUST STOP PLEASE!

Beat.

PATRICIA   Alright.

JEMIMA   I don't like these conversations…

PATRICIA   Okay.

I'm sorry.

A moment.

JEMIMA   I want to be married to him.

PATRICIA   I'm sure you will be.

JEMIMA   He's funny and kind and loyal. He's everything
I should be with.

PATRICIA   Well that's good.

JEMIMA   This is *my* thing.

PATRICIA   Okay.

JEMIMA   For once.

PATRICIA   And I said I'm happy.

JEMIMA   Good.

PATRICIA   You're proper stroppy today.

JEMIMA   I'm not stroppy.

PATRICIA   If I had known you were gonna be stroppy.

JEMIMA   I'm not being stroppy...

PATRICIA   I would have kept my ass home.

JEMIMA   I am stroppy!

PATRICIA   See!

JEMIMA   I really love him Pat.

PATRICIA   I know you do. You're whipped!

JEMIMA   Oh please.

PATRICIA   And you've got your head screwed on in ways that
           I could only ever wish for, I'm proud of you.

JEMIMA   Means a lot.

PATRICIA   Right!

           Enough of all that mooshy shit! When we eating?

JEMIMA   When Mum's back.

PATRICIA   Which is when?

JEMIMA   When she's back innit.

PATRICIA   What did you cook?

JEMIMA   Food!

           Let me even start warming some stuff. (*Heads to
           the kitchen.*)

PATRICIA   Don't burn it you know.

JEMIMA   Funny.

           Beat.

PATRICIA   What's that doing there?!

JEMIMA   What?

PATRICIA   That!

JEMIMA   Don't get it.

PATRICIA   I look like a giraffe.

JEMIMA   You do not.

PATRICIA   Who dug that out?

JEMIMA   Mum?

PATRICIA   Really?

JEMIMA   It's a happy memory.

PATRICIA   Yeah, but…

JEMIMA   It was Dad's birthday.

PATRICIA   I know.

JEMIMA   Think she was going through old pictures.

PATRICIA   And she chose a picture of me to put up?

JEMIMA   And why wouldn't she?

PATRICIA   I dunno…

JEMIMA   She spent years without a single picture in this room, until recently.

PATRICIA   Yeah well.

JEMIMA   I think she wanted to come and visit you.

PATRICIA   Well she didn't.

JEMIMA   Yeah but…

PATRICIA   Don't want…

JEMIMA   I know she wanted to come…

PATRICIA   Yeah / well.

JEMIMA   I see it in her eyes…

PATRICIA   Don't wanna talk about it Jem.

JEMIMA   Fine.

PATRICIA   I get it.

JEMIMA   Do you?

PATRICIA   Ain't the welcome-home party I deserve but...

JEMIMA   Easy now!

PATRICIA   It'll do.

JEMIMA   Look at your head though!

PATRICIA   That's what I'm saying! Long neck!

JEMIMA   You do look like a giraffe.

PATRICIA   Yeah alright!

JEMIMA   We came home and watched *Sister Act* afterwards d'ya remember?

PATRICIA   No.

JEMIMA   Uncle Uchenna's daughters were staying.

PATRICIA   (*Kisses her teeth.*) With their drop lip.

JEMIMA   Why you so rude?

PATRICIA   Where's the lie?

JEMIMA   They grew in to their lips to be fair.

PATRICIA   They needed to.

JEMIMA   Stop it!

PATRICIA   If they weren't so inner...

JEMIMA   They were definitely inner.

PATRICIA   I'd be nicer...

JEMIMA   That's a lie but...

PATRICIA   Definitely a lie.

Beat.

JEMIMA   They mashed up the whole house, guess who cleaned it.

Beat.

PATRICIA   Don't remember much of that year, just remember
            Dad dropped dead.

JEMIMA   God Pat.

PATRICIA   He did!

            He died and that was that.

            Silence.

JEMIMA   Sometimes when I try and think about him, I can't
            see his face, like I had never laid eyes on him
            before, like there was never a memory file of him in
            my brain. I go to bed some nights, literally forcing
            myself to see him, and I wake up and there's
            nothing. Other times, I remember him so clearly.

PATRICIA   I understand that.

            Beat.

JEMIMA   Mum misses him.

PATRICIA   Of course she does.

JEMIMA   I look her sometimes and I worry. When Adam and
            I marry… Like, what does she have to hold on to?

PATRICIA   She'll be fine.

JEMIMA   We can't bring him back, but we can start fresh
            together, right?

PATRICIA   Course sis.

JEMIMA   I feel like my whole world is changing, and I
            know yours is too. But, for the first time in my
            life, I can really see my own path, you know?
            Like, who I am, without the comfort zone. When I
            stand before God and friends, and family, and I
            declare my love for that man, I'll be the happiest
            girl in the world.

PATRICIA   And the most beautiful one.

JEMIMA   When you got out, I swore to myself that I would
            bring you and Mum together again. So I did.

PATRICIA   Who'd of thought it, eh?

JEMIMA   Not me. Didn't think I was brave enough.

PATRICIA   You don't need to be brave.

JEMIMA   I do.

             Pat she… She doesn't know you're here.

             Beat.

PATRICIA   What?

JEMIMA   I mean, this meal, today, you… it was my idea.

PATRICIA   Why would you do that?

JEMIMA   Because I…

PATRICIA   You don't get to decide when it's time.

JEMIMA   But I do, this is my family, you're my family, we
             are a family… even though Dad has gone, and he
             will never see me walk down the aisle…

PATRICIA   No, this isn't about you.

JEMIMA   It's about all of us.

PATRICIA   No Jem, you should have left well alone.

JEMIMA   She needs to see you.

PATRICIA   That's her decision not yours.

JEMIMA   But look how far you've come.

PATRICIA   Yes I have and I don't need any setbacks.

JEMIMA   And it won't be.

PATRICIA   You don't know that.

JEMIMA   You've changed.

PATRICIA   I haven't changed.

JEMIMA   You know what I mean.

PATRICIA   No, I didn't need to change I needed to get better.

JEMIMA   That's what I meant.

PATRICIA   That's not what you said.

JEMIMA   Trust me.

PATRICIA   I can't deal with any madness today Jem.

JEMIMA   It will be fine.

PATRICIA   You don't know that.

JEMIMA   I do.

PATRICIA   Fine.

             PATRICIA *sits*.

             JEMIMA *checks on the food*.

JEMIMA   (*Sings*.) I sing because I'm happy…

PATRICIA   No thanks.

JEMIMA   (*Sings*.) And I sing, because I'm free.

PATRICIA   I know what you're doing.

JEMIMA   (*Sings*.) His eye is on the sparrow.

             Signals to PATRICIA *to join in but she doesn't.*

             (*Sings*.) His eye is on the sparrow.

             Signals again.

             (*Sings*.) And I know he watches…

             She waits.

             (*Sings*.) And I know he watches –

             Waits.

PATRICIA   (*Sings*.) And I know he watches –

JEMIMA /   (*Singing*.) Meee.
PATRICIA

             They repeat.

             *They get caught up in the moment, singing and
             laughing uncontrollably.*

MAMA *enters the space, her hands full with groceries. She sees* PATRICIA *and freezes. Watches them.*

PATRICIA *sees her. Stops singing. They stare into each other. No one moves.*

Lights down.

Humming sounds.

Scene Three

A different time.

A different space.

Humming continues.

PATRICIA   It rained today. Hard. Cleansing us of our past, renewing us, making good again.

Soaked all the way through, I wonder if it's raining for you too. If the sky opened its blinds and cried all over you too.

I wonder if the sky watches over you and guides you as you look up for me.

Does it show you my face, do you even remember me?

Does it smile for you when you're feeling blue?

Wrap you in arms made of clouds, so soft, I wonder if you even knew that my heart it beats only for you.

Do you get to smell freshly cut grass and run around in the park, arms flapping high and low, free in your soul, free to roam this earth any which way your body rolls. I wonder if you know, that every night before I close my eyes I sing to you.

Sweet little angel of mine I sing to you, the purest of notes from my heart straight to yours.

I wonder if you know that the curl of your lips is imprinted in the deepest depths of my being. Do you know how I miss you little angel? Do you know?

JEMIMA*'s voice sounds from different space.*

JEMIMA   It's getting cold Pat.

A different space.

PATRICIA   (*Whispers.*) When you need me look up, the sky will show you my face.

A different space.

JEMIMA   Pat.

Lights interrupt her.

Kitchen.

Dining table.

Scene Four

MAMA *and* JEMIMA *are seated.*

JEMIMA   PAT IT'S GETTING COLD.

PATRICIA   Sorry.

She pulls up a seat.

They dish in silence.

JEMIMA   Drinks anyone?

PATRICIA   I've got water, thank you.

JEMIMA   Mum?

MAMA   You cut your hair.

Beat.

PATRICIA   No.

JEMIMA   Shall I pour for you?

MAMA   It doesn't suit your face.

PATRICIA   I didn't.

JEMIMA   Mama?

MAMA   Water's fine.

She pours.

JEMIMA   This is nice.

MAMA   You look better when it frames your face.

PATRICIA   I haven't cut it Mum…

JEMIMA   Looks great.

MAMA   Looks shorter…

PATRICIA   Well it's not…

MAMA   Looks it…

JEMIMA   I'm sure… I'm sure it's not.

PATRICIA   Probably broke…

JEMIMA   You should get it braided.

PATRICIA   Nah, my hair likes freedom.

JEMIMA   You can still have that with braids.

MAMA   You're not looking after your hair?

PATRICIA   I try.

JEMIMA   I'll get my hairdresser to sort you out good.

PATRICIA   No thank you!

JEMIMA   She's great you'd like her.

MAMA   You're looking thin.

PATRICIA   Am I?

JEMIMA   Mum she's always been little.

MAMA   I hope you're eating well, wherever you're living.

PATRICIA   I am.

JEMIMA   She's in Catford now Mum.

PATRICIA   Yeah, small but cosy.

            Beat.

MAMA   Good.

PATRICIA   I… I bought you some tulips.

MAMA   Thank you.

PATRICIA   I seem to have misplaced them.

JEMIMA   It's the thought that counts.

MAMA   Next time.

PATRICIA   They were for your birthday… So.

MAMA   This is nice enough.

JEMIMA   Patricia has been so busy with interviews and…

MAMA   Interviews?

PATRICIA   Yeah, all's going well.

MAMA   Well I'm glad to hear it.

PATRICIA   I'd love you to come visit.

MAMA   Oh, I'm sure we can arrange that one day.

PATRICIA   I could get you a cab if…

MAMA   Oh no / no.

PATRICIA   I mean if you don't want…

MAMA   It's not that I…

PATRICIA   I could cook…

MAMA   You can cook?

PATRICIA   Training to be a chef actually, well… That's the
            plan. I've already taken one exam.

MAMA   Well… well done.

PATRICIA   So, I'll cook some time… Maybe?

MAMA   Maybe.

JEMIMA   Carrot cake when you're ready Mum.

PATRICIA   Yum.

MAMA   I can't have too much!

JEMIMA   Oh come on!

MAMA   These people you have making you cakes are trying to kill you slowly.

JEMIMA   Don't be ridiculous.

MAMA   It's true.

JEMIMA   Mum, just eat the cake and stop overanalysing.

MAMA   I am not overanalysing anything.

PATRICIA   I love carrot cake.

MAMA   You yourself should be careful.

PATRICIA   Sorry, when it comes to cake I can't be.

MAMA   When you were five years old the school called your father and I because you were running around calling yourself a choo-choo train and banging your head into walls.

JEMIMA   What?

MAMA   It's true, and throwing yourself about like you were indestructible.

PATRICIA   You never told me that before.

MAMA   I did.

PATRICIA   I'd remember that Mum.

MAMA   Are you calling me a liar.

JEMIMA   No.

MAMA   Am I speaking with you?

PATRICIA   I can't remember Mum.

JEMIMA   Me neither.

MAMA   Did anyone ask you yourself Jemima. Did I ask you if you can remember?

JEMIMA   No...

MAMA   Well then close your mouth and stop answering like your sister does not have her own lips and her own brain.

Beat.

Cut me small cake.

JEMIMA   Thought so!

MAMA   I don't need you to discuss it with me either.

JEMIMA   Wouldn't dream of it!

JEMIMA *gets up and carefully pulls the cake out of the fridge, places it in front of them.*

MAMA   Bring me napkin.

JEMIMA   Yes madam!

MAMA   You will need a sharper knife than this also.

She searches for one.

I don't know why you are collecting cakes from these same people after your last cake.

PATRICIA   What happened with the last cake?

MAMA   There was hair all over it.

JEMIMA   (*From the kitchen.*) There was not.

MAMA   I saw it with my own eyes.

JEMIMA *returns.*

JEMIMA   Here we go.

MAMA   Will I cut my own cake?

JEMIMA   Nobody asked you to!

MAMA   Where are my candles?

JEMIMA   I asked Patricia to pick some up.

PATRICIA   What?!

MAMA   Typical!

PATRICIA   She asked me nothing of the kind.

MAMA   Are you calling your sister a liar?

PATRICIA   Yes!

MAMA   So you came here empty-handed and could not be bothered to get me candles for my birthday cake?

JEMIMA   She's joking!

            MAMA *laughs quietly to herself.*

MAMA   You have forgotten the look on your mother's face when she is playing small tricks on you.

PATRICIA   I don't recall my mother playing tricks on me.

            JEMIMA *pulls out a large chest from behind the sofa. It is wrapped in a bow.*

JEMIMA   Well what do we have here?

MAMA   What is this?

JEMIMA   Why don't you open up and have a look.

MAMA   I don't like this one.

JEMIMA   Pat grab the champagne glasses from the top-right cupboard, and the Shloer… just there see.

MAMA   (*Points.*) Am I supposed to remove this bow?

JEMIMA   Hurry up Mother!

PATRICIA   Here you go.

JEMIMA   On the table will do… Mum you have ten seconds to open this! Ten.

            MAMA *tries to unwrap with speed.*

            Five.

PATRICIA   Five?

JEMIMA   Shut up!

MAMA   You have wrapped this as tight as you can!

She opens the chest and stands silent.

JEMIMA   ONE!!!

Happy birthday Mum!!!

MAMA *doesn't move.*

MAMA   Where did you find these things?

JEMIMA   Boxes you'd hidden in the attic, photo albums
you'd left without memories.

MAMA   It's beautiful.

JEMIMA   I just thought, as you prepare to make more
memories with the newest addition to the family,
you should be able to look back on the old with
ease.

MAMA   Thank you.

Beat.

JEMIMA   I'll say it again, as you prepare to make more
memories with the *newest* member of the family…

The penny slowly drops.

MAMA   (*Overcome by excitement.*) No!!!

JEMIMA   (*Giggles.*) Yes Ma!

MAMA   Jesus is my God! Hey! Chineke!

*She claps her hands and sings short prayer in
Igbo as she approaches* JEMIMA.

You're expecting a child. You and Adam are with
child?

JEMIMA   We are with child!!!

MAMA   Hey!!!

MAMA *claps her hands together and runs over and hugs* JEMIMA. *They laugh.*

JEMIMA   Happy birthday Grandma.

PATRICIA *watches on.*

MAMA   How far?

JEMIMA   Twelve nearly thirteen weeks.

MAMA   And you have hidden this from me all this time?

JEMIMA   I wanted to wait until your birthday.

MAMA   Oh! I must call everybody.

JEMIMA   Can we wait?

MAMA   You are right!

JEMIMA   I am?

MAMA   Not everybody has good intentions, you will be telling them your great news and they will be visiting witch doctor to take away your good fortunate.

JEMIMA   Alright Mum!

MAMA   It is true. Don't be going to that boy's compound until your baby is of strong age.

JEMIMA   Enough thank you!

MAMA   I have not met all of his family to adequately form an opinion on their character.

JEMIMA   If you say so!!

MAMA   (*Sings as she clears the table.*) My God is so good, my God is so good, my God is so good, my God is so good.

PATRICIA   Congratulations Jem.

JEMIMA   Thank you.

PATRICIA   You didn't say earlier?

JEMIMA   I know!

PATRICIA   It's good anyway, you obviously wanted to wait…

JEMIMA   I did.

PATRICIA   It's great… it's really great.

MAMA *returns*.

MAMA   Where is Adam?

JEMIMA   He should be back home by now.

MAMA   He should be coming here and greeting me.

JEMIMA   Today's about the three of us Mum. I wanted to share this news with the two of you, in the same room. January has… January has always been a painful month for Patricia / … And us.

PATRICIA   You don't need to do that babe…

JEMIMA   It's always been. And I guess I wanted to help change that.

PATRICIA   Great.

MAMA   Let's toast one more time!

MAMA *tops up*.

PATRICIA   I'm not feeling too great.

MAMA   What's wrong?

PATRICIA   Erm, it's probably nothing, just a big or… I should… I should get off.

JEMIMA   Wait a while.

PATRICIA   Honestly it's…

MAMA   What do you feel.

PATRICIA   My head…

MAMA   I have paracetomol.

PATRICIA   I'll be fine, I just need to get home and lie down.

MAMA   You can lie upstairs.

PATRICIA   Honestly…

JEMIMA   Honestly what Pat?

PATRICIA   I'd just… look I'd just like to go now… I can't…
            I can't do this.

MAMA   Do what? What can't you do?

JEMIMA   Is it me?

PATRICIA   No.

JEMIMA   Is this all too soon.

PATRICIA   I don't know Jem.

MAMA   When you should be happy for your sister you are
            busy causing drama.

JEMIMA   It's fine.

PATRICIA   I don't want to argue with you Mum.

MAMA   Argue with me? Why would you be arguing with
            me?

PATRICIA   I'm just… I'm just not feeling good.

MAMA   And you don't want to do the things that can help
            you feel better.

PATRICIA   (*Points towards the box.*) That… In there, is the
            dress I put her in before we left her.

JEMIMA   What?

MAMA   It's not the same dress.

PATRICIA   I know what she was wearing, I have replayed it
            every day since we flew back home.

JEMIMA   I… I'm sorry Pat I thought it was one of ours.

PATRICIA   It's fine.

MAMA   And you will be punishing me now?

PATRICIA   No Mum.

MAMA	You will go back and tell your support worker that you were ill-treated here.
PATRICIA	I was ill-treated here.
JEMIMA	Pat what are you doing?
PATRICIA	This is too much for me Jem. These walls. This room… All of this is too much today.
MAMA	Then you should go home and feel better.
JEMIMA	Mum stop it. Pat take your time, go, I'll call you soon.
MAMA	So she can make you feel worse?
JEMIMA	Stop.
PATRICIA	Do you see me Mum?
MAMA	What kind of question is that?
PATRICIA	Can you see I'm better.
MAMA	I'm not having this conversation with you.
PATRICIA	Well I am. I am better… clearer.
JEMIMA	And we're proud of you.
PATRICIA	I'm going to get in touch with her soon.
MAMA	No.
JEMIMA	Mum.
MAMA	You have no business interfering in her life at this stage.
PATRICIA	How can you say that?
MAMA	Leave well alone.
PATRICIA	All is not well.
MAMA	Leave her alone, she is happy.
PATRICIA	How would you know?
MAMA	I know.

Beat.

JEMIMA	How?
MAMA	I am not at liberty to be overexplaining myself today.
PATRICIA	You speak to them.
MAMA	I am going to rest myself now.
PATRICIA	No.
MAMA	I will be happy to talk to you another day.
PATRICIA	No.
JEMIMA	Mum, you speak to Baby?
PATRICIA	Answer her.
MAMA	I send money every month as I always have done.
JEMIMA	That wasn't my question.
MAMA	Patricia you have returned to antagonise me.
JEMIMA	Don't do that Mum.
MAMA	Will you blame me for the sky changing colour at night?
JEMIMA	Give Patricia the contact details.
MAMA	There is no excuse for you to be addressing me anyhow in my home.
JEMIMA	Give it to her.
MAMA	You should stop talking now.
JEMIMA	There is a child growing inside of me that I will never allow you to see whilst you behave like this.
MAMA	What did you say to me?
JEMIMA	You can't treat her like this.
MAMA	And what of me and all I have had to go through on my own. What of the times that your sister ransacked my home, brought her criminal friends to take solace in my home, what of the times she

attacked and antagonised our friends. What of the time she raised her hands to her own mother. She is damaged.

JEMIMA   I don't recognise you.

MAMA   And I don't recognise you.

You have decided to morph yourself into your sister.

PATRICIA   I don't want to fight.

MAMA   You have ruined my birthday.

PATRICIA   I didn't mean for that to happen.

MAMA   You will not talk to me anyhow in my own home.

You will go outside now and you will tell your people I threw you outside...

PATRICIA   No...

MAMA   ... And that is why you are not welcome in my home, that is why you can take your bad ways and carry them outside with you.

PATRICIA   They told me not to come and see you yet you know.

MAMA   Well you should carry your belongings and go and see them.

JEMIMA   You will listen to her.

PATRICIA   I woke up this morning and the sun beamed through my window, I was coming home to see my mother, she had asked for me to come home, I bought flowers... replayed all the ways I would hug you when I first saw you... I ain't touched you in like five years and it's nothing to you... I'm doing good Mum.

MAMA   I am happy for you.

PATRICIA   Really?

MAMA   Yes really.

PATRICIA   Fifteen years nearly to the day and I remember
            what her breath smells like, how it felt on my
            cheek.

MAMA   I can't hear this.

PATRICIA   I would have given anything for you to have held
            me like you just held Jemima.

MAMA   Your sister is engaged to be wed and is a grown
            woman. What kind of nonsense must be at play in
            your head for you to compare yourself at that age
            and Jemima now.

JEMIMA   That's not the point Mum.

MAMA   What is the point? Enlighten me.

            I am obviously such a bad mother.

PATRICIA   I didn't say that.

MAMA   Carry yourself home if you feel that way.

JEMIMA   Let's all calm down.

MAMA   No.

PATRICIA   This must be hard for you.

MAMA   I am not responsible for the demons that lie within
            you.

JEMIMA   Pat I'm so sorry.

PATRICIA   Must be hard Mum.

MAMA   Stop saying that.

PATRICIA   Why do you hate me?

MAMA   You want me to hate you so you can run and tell
            everybody what a horrible mother I am.

PATRICIA   I came back to start afresh Mum. I'm on the right
            track.

MAMA   Good.

PATRICIA   I don't want to fight. I want to be part of your life.

MAMA   I am happy for you.

PATRICIA   Are you hearing me?

MAMA   I am hearing you.

Beat.

PATRICIA   I want us to be in each other's lives.

MAMA   Patricia I don't want to get into all of this now.

PATRICIA   You don't want to.

MAMA   I never said that.

PATRICIA   You don't have to.

MAMA   Patricia I'm tired.

PATRICIA   The whole time I was inside...

MAMA   I said I don't want to talk about this...

PATRICIA   You never came Mum.

MAMA   Why would I come?

PATRICIA   So I would know you still cared...

MAMA   You smashed up this house.

PATRICIA   Don't say that Mum.

MAMA   You want me to come and visit you after the destruction you left behind?

PATRICIA   I'm better.

MAMA   You were not sick. You are cursed.

PATRICIA   Don't say that.

MAMA   You are cursed.

JEMIMA   Mum, you can't say things like that I won't allow / you to say things like that.

PATRICIA   So cursed, so bad, so evil. I will never do to my daughter what you have done to me.

MAMA   You don't have a daughter.

PATRICIA   I'm going to find her Mum.

MAMA   You will do well to leave that one alone.

PATRICIA   So she can think I sent her away like you have
            consistently done with me.

MAMA   I never sent you away, / you chose to live that life
            and so you had to go and see it out.

PATRICIA   You allowed these people to turn you against your
            own child and you sent her away, you sent me
            away and made me leave her. The one good thing
            I ever had you / made me leave her.

MAMA   Stop talking, stop talking now.

            Thirty-two years of shame, that's what you have
            given me. Me your mother, with all the sacrifices
            I have made for you. And you walk back into this
            house today after you let them lock you up like an
            animal that had not been raised right.

PATRICIA   Okay enough!

MAMA   There was a storm that day.

            It rained for a whole week. Floods everywhere.
            Trees fell... people died and your father...

PATRICIA   Don't bring my father up... don't...

MAMA   ... couldn't find my bag, he didn't even know that
            I had one.

JEMIMA   Enough Mum, stop talking now, stop... Mum
            please.

MAMA   ... somehow we made it... Nineteen hours... you
            refused to turn so we waited nineteen hours until
            they decided to cut you out... You turned blue...
            I cried... your father cried... we all cried but
            you... Defiant... stubborn. Refused to breathe life
            into your own lungs. Made us wait until you were
            ready. When you cried we rejoiced... our

firstborn... alive by some miracle... but they wouldn't let me hold you... they took you... so small... all those tubes... so helpless... all of us... when you came home you cried every day non-stop for a whole year crying crying crying.

When your father would hold you you would smile fall asleep in his arms everything your father said you would do both a daughter and a wife... / even at death he was with you...

PATRICIA   Stop talking about him.

MAMA   You have been disturbed your whole life... in birth... in youth and now here... today... the devil enters into my home...

PATRICIA   I'm the / devil's child Mum... I'm so evil, so disgusting, I'm the scummiest evil child ever to cross this earth! I'm so terrible.

MAMA   ... but Jesus reigns over this house. No weapon shall prosper whilst under the roof of this house. In Jesus' name. I banish all ill in Jesus' name. I rebuke your disease in Jesus' name. I won't allow it! I won't allow you to ruin her life do you hear me... DO YOU HEAR ME!

    MAMA *goes towards* PATRICIA.

PATRICIA   You cannot shame me any more.

MAMA   DO YOU HEAR ME?

PATRICIA   I hear you.

MAMA   All these people... your daughter she is ill your daughter she has mental something or other... you let these people tell you you have mental problems... I looked after you, I looked after all of you, why would you want to punish me in this way?

    Silence.

PATRICIA   We were in prayer group...

    I don't think you were ever told fully.

MAMA *does not move.*

There were ten of us...

He would sit with me every Wednesday. Are you hearing me?

Ask me questions as he led Bible study for his father. After he would ask what I'd do when I got home, we would talk about JLo and Puff Daddy make up raps and sing... we would laugh and play-fight... hands finding places on my body I didn't even know existed...

He would tickle me until my lungs ached I would giggle when I knew I shouldn't... We would pray as he took away the very last part of purity I had... There would always be a point where he would find himself entwined / in me...

MAMA *grabs her Bible from the shelf, flicks through and begins repeating the following, and then begins praying through song.* PATRICIA *continues speaking over this.*

MAMA   'No weapon that is formed against you will prosper; and every tongue that accuses you in judgement you will condemn. This is the heritage of the servants of the Lord, And their vindication is from Me.'

PATRICIA ... flesh brushing upon my flesh... a hand on a knee a hand resting next to my leg index finger stroking my thigh... and I wouldn't stop him... I had no right to stop him. Do as he says you always told me, this wasn't any different... I'd just sit there. Still. Every time. Every Wednesday every study evening... in this house... wherever we were... I'd just close my eyes and stay still...

MAMA *continues praying/singing.*

Obedient, respectful, dutiful, God-fearing... I'd remain still... I begged you to believe me... choose me... help me... stay in the house you told

me… hide my shame you told me… but she was
not shame… a butterfly… my butterfly… they told
me not to come, you're not ready Patricia, we will
arrange a social worker Patricia…

But I woke up this morning and the sun beamed
through my window, the day inviting me to taste
all it had to offer. A new dawn a new opportunity
to collect my slice of life my special gift. You
don't have to ever see me again Mum.

MAMA *stops singing*.

You don't even have to love me but… a butterfly
landed on my shoulder when I didn't even know
I still had a limb to feel the gust of its wings…
and I want to feel that again… are you listening to
me Mum.

MAMA *has made her way over to the sofa where
she is struggling to regulate her breathing*.

Mum.

MAMA   Some water please.

           JEMIMA *doesn't move*.

PATRICIA   Did you hear anything I just said?

MAMA   Water Jemima.

           JEMIMA *doesn't move*.

PATRICIA   What's wrong with her?

           JEMIMA *doesn't respond*.

MAMA   Water please.

PATRICIA   Jemima.

           PATRICIA *grabs a glass from the cabinet and
           pours water for her mother.*

MAMA   Top cupboard on the left, there's a blue pill packet.

           PATRICIA *grabs this and brings both over to her
           mother.*

Thank you.

MAMA *struggles to breathe.*

PATRICIA   Call an ambulance.

Slowly PATRICIA *approaches* MAMA, *lifts her head, places it on her lap and stokes her hair.*

Jemima call an ambulance.

JEMIMA   Okay.

JEMIMA *runs out.*

PATRICIA *rocks* MAMA.

MAMA   Pat.

PATRICIA   It's okay Mum.

MAMA   I am your mother.

PATRICIA   Try not to speak.

MAMA   It is my job to protect you.

Beat.

PATRICIA *continues to comfort* MAMA. *Rocks her slowly.*

Lights down.

The End.

AMONGST THE REEDS

Chino Odimba

Characters

ONI, *seventeen-year-old Nigerian girl*
GILLIAN, *sixteen- to seventeen-year-old Vietnamese girl; she is heavily pregnant*

Both have an accent that is distinct and clear.

Setting

1. A desk is visible with two sleeping bags sprawled out underneath it. Two garden chairs sit at either end of the table. There are two Ghana-must-go bags sitting in a corner with clothes hanging out of them. A small, barely functioning, stereo sits on the table. There is a can of Coke and a bag of sweets on the table. Along the walls there is a variety of lamps, candles in jars and lights that light up the space. The walls are covered in ripped and cut-out pictures and pages of magazines of Black women's hairstyles.

2. A Perspex box with a desk – brightly lit by strip lights.

3. Another Perspex box with a sofa, a coffee table and children's toys – also lit with strip lights.

Note on Text

… indicates a trailing off at the end of a sentence or a pause

/ indicates an overlap in speech between two characters or within a character's dialogue

A new paragraph indicates a natural pause or change of thought in dialogue

This text went to press before the end of rehearsals and so may differ slightly from the play as performed

Scene One

That day.

GILLIAN *peers out of the dirty slats of a broken window blind. She is in semi-darkness. A strong ray of light pushes into the darkness.*

Beat.

GILLIAN   It is like a…

It is like when…

Everything…

Everything is making a sound.

Stretching up, waking up.

GILLIAN *stares hard at the outside world –*

And the smell of it…

Can you smell it?

Imagine that.

The smell of grass and the road melting.

I am almost smelling it…

Or the smell of flowers.

Big yellow flowers.

And their small petals.

Like the perfume your mother is wearing.

I miss the smell of things opening and reaching for the light.

I miss those things and if I could just see…

Beat.

Should I go to see?

Feel it?

I want to reach out to the light too.

Like those flowers.

Oni?

Should I go?

ONI *appears out of a dark corner of the room* –

Oni?

Oni say something.

Should we go?

ONI   Stay here wiff me.

GILLIAN   If I see it…

Then I will…

ONI   What? What will change Gill-li-an?

GILLIAN   Can you not smell it? Do you not want to put your head on the grass and feel the heat on your face? That warmness on your face and the sound of bees and flies in your ears /

ONI   I do not like bees /

GILLIAN   Can you not hear the ice-cream van?

Listen.

It is getting closer.

Do you not want to just run out there before…

Before it goes…

Can you hear that?

Beat.

The silence after…

Like the sound of happiness leaving and no one knows what to do.

I want to run after it /

ONI   You would do dat? Run out dere?

Juss like dat? /

GILLIAN   I didn't say that Oni.

I want to imagine /

ONI   But you think about it for ar second?

You want to try /

GILLIAN   No /

ONI   I think you should Gill-li-an. Go on try it.

Go to de door and juss open it.

Go down de stairs out into de street.

Walk down de street like you ar juss anodder parson going about deer business. Maybe for one day or two. Maybe more. But one day juss like dat /

GILLIAN   I don't say I want to /

ONI   If you go out dere you know what will happen.

GILLIAN   I know.

Just to imagine /

ONI   Before seven? Before time? Before de dark?

GILLIAN   I know /

ONI   It won't matter what you see.

Dey will see you.

GILLIAN   Yes but when was the last time you sat outside eating ice cream?

On the first real day of summer /

ONI   I do not like summer.

             Beat.

             Move away from de window Gill-li-an.

             Move from dere /

GILLIAN   Why? Why are you always telling me what to do?

ONI   Think of de baby.

GILLIAN   I just want to imagine /

ONI   I am bored of all your talking /

GILLIAN   I am bored of your face!

             Short beat.

             No one can see me.

             GILLIAN *takes a seat at the table –*

             Beat.

             ONI *moves towards her –*

ONI   What is your name?

GILLIAN   Gillian /

ONI   Nice name. My name is Oni. O-Nee.

             Can you pronounce?

             It means born on holy ground.

             Because I was born outside de church. My modder
             was praying in church one Sunday and den
             suddenly I want to come out. When she went
             outside to get some air, I juss dropped out dere on
             de ground. My fadder was dere and said it was
             like I came out running.

             GILLIAN *lets a little smile slip –*

             Is baby's fadder here?

GILLIAN   He is coming for us.

ONI   He is young like you?

GILLIAN   I am not a child /

ONI   What is de colour of his hair?

             Is he fit?

             I bet he have blue eyes…

GILLIAN   He have eyes that make you want to faint. When
             he look at you with those eyes…

             He will come for us. Me and baby. Maybe not
             now. Maybe not for a while.

             *ONI walks away and comes back with two mugs –
             one has a broken handle.*

             She places a cup in front of GILLIAN, *and takes a
             seat.*

ONI   Drink it. I have put lots of sugar.

GILLIAN   I don't have any money /

ONI   Don't worry about dat. Today I do two women's
             hair. Two. One after de odder. One girlfriend's har
             hair was like trying to plait peppercorn.

             Dey say me 'You're so much better den de
             hairdressers.' I say dem 'Oh good' but no tell
             anybody. Shsssh!

             ONI mockingly puts a finger to her lips –

             Dey think I am grown woman too. If they know I
             am juss seventeen den dey try to pay you less
             money.

             Beat.

             You want me to buy you cake?

             Cake is not good for you anyway. Fruit is better /

GILLIAN   I like cake.

ONI   I like cake too.

             Beat.

Why were you standing dere?

I see you and think you look so / too beautiful for street girlfriend /

GILLIAN   I don't think so. I am wearing same jeans for four days. No shower, no make-up and shoe broken from running.

ONI   Running from ware?

Who are you running from?

Beat.

ONI *glances down at* GILLIAN*'s feet* –

Jelly shoes not good look yeah girlfriend /

GILLIAN   Only shoe I was wearing that day I run. Since then be sleeping in front of big department store.

ONI *kneels down to take off* GILLIAN*'s shoes* –

ONI   I am thinking awww look at dat little Chinese girlfriend selling Prada at wrong time in wrong place /

GILLIAN   I am not Chinese.

ONI   Vietnam yeah girlfriend…

Well you ar very lucky den dat you meet your girlfriend Oni. Oni be de only girlfriend you need on street.

ONI *does a kind of superhero pose* –

GILLIAN*'s face melts into a smile* –

Stay wiff me. I will find someware warm and safe for you and…

ONI *leans into* GILLIAN *to whisper to her* –

Let me tell you something I don't tell everyone.

You won't tell anyone?

GILLIAN *shakes her head* –

I come from ar family of traditional midwives. Do you know dis one?

You know helping woman give barth? My mother, har mother and har mother before har have all been doing dis one.

Anyway girlfriend de thing be dis. I can see from juss looking at your belly wedder it is boy or girl and if I touch it, even better, den I can tell you wedder your baby going to be good person, bad person, or priest.

GILLIAN   Now?

ONI   Anyway I do not need to touch it to tell you dis one. It is ar girl. Ar beautiful girl and I am seeing something like har fingers. Dey ar going to be long long...

GILLIAN   Long fingers?

           ONI *closes her eyes for a second –*

           What?

ONI   Don't panic. I am juss seeing something /

GILLIAN   Tell me.

ONI   I can see har Gill-li-an. Dis baby har hair is long. So long. I am seeing baby and she is running around singing and playing.

           Beat.

           You see if we can stay in my new place for long enuff and de baby come out happy helltee baby den I know dat my own luck change. And once I have my leave to remain...

           Me and you and baby we can have everything we want. I can go to college and study to be the best midwife... And you and baby...

GILLIAN   She is happy?

ONI   Like de happiest small girlfriend...

             I think about will de nice lovely hair I am doing
             on baby. I have de fastest fingers any woman has
             had on har head. One week twist, one week
             cornrow, anodder week juss like wavy extensions.
             Har is going to be de baddest Vietnamesey
             girlfriend. De most beautiful one.

             I mean it Gill-li-an.

             ONI *pulls a neatly folded picture out of her*
             pocket. She opens it out –

             It is for you.

             I can be your best girlfriend.

             I think dis ar special baby. Har is ar kind of spirit
             child. You know dis one? When you have baby
             like dat you can have anything you want /

GILLIAN   I don't want anything else Oni. I just want baby. I
             just want to keep my baby. I just want to see her
             long fingers, and her long hair and I want to see
             her laughing like you say. Just like that. Please.
             Just like that.

             ONI *moves to the window/blinds –*

ONI   If you want dat den you have to stop worrying
             about what is out dere.

             What is out dere...

             You won't see it coming. You won't even know it
             is dere. Dey will juss come for you. Like ar big
             bird in de sky, dey will come. And it won't be you
             dey want. It will be baby. Dey will come like ar
             flash, wiff deer dark eyes and heavy breting and
             take your baby. Take har someware else ware you
             can nevar see har ageen.

             Dis place Gill-li-an, is our place ware dey won't
             see us. Like long grass and reeds shaking wiff de
             wind, dey can't see us. Dey will try but here

amongst de reeds, we can be juss be like little animals crawling on our bellies, waiting for dat big bird in de sky to go arway.

We do not belong out dere.

Daytime is not for us /

GILLIAN   Why do you say that?

Why you always say these things to me?

ONI   Can you not see Gill-li-an? Your baby is like de sign / de light dat dey are waiting to see. If you want us to keep on living /

GILLIAN   Living? /

ONI   Yes!

GILLIAN   Who will see us if we go for one ice cream?

Maybe go to seaside?

We can wear bikini, and put flowers in our hair.

ONI   Bikini?

Gill-li-an /

GILLIAN   Can you imagine me in a bikini? Or swimming?

GILLIAN pushes her bump out further –

I sink. I sink to the bottom of the sea.

The two girls burst out into laughter –

ONI   I would save you /

GILLIAN   You can't swim /

ONI   I would call lifeguard /

GILLIAN   And that poor lifeguard will have to carry me and baby /

ONI   And give you de kiss of life /

GILLIAN   With tongues /

ONI   Dat is really disgusting Gill-li-an /

GILLIAN   Kiss me until he has sucked all the water from my
             mouth.

             GILLIAN *exaggerates the sound of kissing –*

ONI   I don't like when you talk like dis /

GILLIAN   You have never been kissed that's why.

ONI   I have plenty boyfriend before /

GILLIAN   Where? What's their name? Show me picture /

ONI   Why you don't juss believe me? Why ar you
             asking question about everything today?

             I ever lie to you before Gill-li-an? In all dis time
             you find one lie I tell you?

             If you no want to believe me any more den maybe
             I can go now /

GILLIAN   You can't!

             Beat.

ONI   –

GILLIAN   Oni?

             Short beat.

             Will I ever feel the sun on my face again Oni?

             Lights –

Scene Two

Four months before that day.

ONI *is in her Perspex box.*

ONI   My name is Beatrice Oni Agbede.

You can see it dere. I am juss waiting for you to give me leave to remain. My solicitor told me to come here. She said that you have news for me about my application.

You believe me now don't you? You believe that I am not ar adult now don't you?

Did you speak to de headmistress at St Mary's School. Did she tell you what ar good student I used to be. Har favourite. She will have told you by now what year I was dere, maybe she even send de papers wiff my barth date?

I use my last one pound for bus juss to get here...

What is it?

Why are you looking at me like dat?

It is de same way dey look at me dat day aftar I go to police. But now you are looking at me like dis?

Beat.

What do you mean? Why do you want me to sign dere?

I am seventeen. I am seventeen...

Ask my school ageen. If I had my passport I would show you but she has taken everything from me.

Short beat.

What about my application? You can see dat can't you?

I ask you for help. You are meant to be helping me
now. I tell dem, my solicitor, the officers
everythin' about Auntie. I tell I run from har
house. Scared for my life. I tell dem street no good
but when someone hit your head wiff high-heel
shoe, burn you wiff iron and...

And I ask them –

Do you know what Scotch bonnet feel like in your
eye?

Who saw me? Who saw me enter dis country?
Who saw me living in dat back room for months?
Dis place dat is full of people you nevar see.

Please. I did not want to run away and do dis
shame. She bring me here promising my modder
she will look aftar me. She said dat to har. My
kind auntie. Instead she find every excuse to beat
me. Becuss har daughter's hair was not neat
enough for school, becuss it is not clean enuff
behind de toilet becuss becuss...

Please. Please you can't do dis!

If I go back I will shame my family. Do you not
understand? If I go back dere is nothing for me to
imagine any more. Everything will be over for me.
I have wasted my only chance to do something
good.

Please will you get someone. I know someone will
have to believe me. I don't mind what odder tests
you want to do. Please.

Please. I have never kissed ar boy. Never. I am ar
virgin. You can do test. I am juss ar girl. I am ar
good girl.

Beat.

Can you hear me?

Please leave me alone.

Ware are you taking me?

Please… I am juss ar girl.

The lights go out in the Perspex box.

Scene Three

That day.

The window is now covered by bits of the papers that were previously on the walls.

GILLIAN *is reaching up trying to remove a poster she can't quite reach from the wall. She drags one of the chairs across the room. She stands on it. The chair wobbles.*

ONI *appears.*

ONI	What am I seeing?
GILLIAN	I didn't want to wake you up /
ONI	You want to be doing everythin' on your own now?
GILLIAN	This place /
ONI	You don't need Oni?
GILLIAN	I need to make it ready /
ONI	It is dangerous /
GILLIAN	Make it clean /
ONI	It looks okay Gill-li-an /
GILLIAN	For baby. I think we can maybe put pictures of baby here /
ONI	What about dis pictures? You don't care about hairstyles any more?
	Dere's plenty of space for baby photo.

Here and here…

GILLIAN   I am moving pictures. Not throwing them away.
            Just moving them and…

GILLIAN scrambles down –

*She reaches into a bag and pulls out a bit of paper.
She reaches under the table and pulls at a ball of
Blue-Tack. She walks over to one of the windows
and tacks the piece of paper to the wall – another
picture of a Black woman's hairstyle –*

ONI   Oh my god!! Oh my god!! Oh my god!

GILLIAN   You like?

ONI   Like? Like? I am loving dis one girlfriend. How
            did you find it?

ONI rushes over to the poster –

*She strokes the image. She glides her hands across
the whole picture.*

I think I want to scream or somethin'. My
girlfriend Gill-li-an always have my back. Always
know how to make Oni happy always juss so on it
Gill-li-an.

(*Pointing at poster.*) You wouldn't know dat was
ar weave would you? Why is it dat I find de best
girlfriend on de street like dis? How is it dat I am
so lucky like dis?

Ware did you get dis one from?

GILLIAN   I was calling you /

ONI   Dat doesn't matter now /

GILLIAN   I think maybe we have to leave this place now?

ONI   Why?

            What's happened?

            We don't need to go anywhere.

            No one knows we are here.

I have only seen one parson come here in four months. Dey didn't even get past de front door becuss it was too dark. Imagine if we were as scared of de dark as dem.

Dis is de best place to stay.

GILLIAN   We can find somewhere else.

Without mould and mice.

For baby /

ONI   Someware else now?

Why Gill-li-an?

Beat.

Let's dance dat will cheer you up.

ONI *excitedly bounces around the room –*

Imagine Gill-li-an. Imagine we ar at ar very big party wiff lots of famous people like Diana Ross. Imagine Gill-li-an, I have de highest heels on and I am dancing wiff I don't know. Erm…

GILLIAN *goes to sit on a chair –*

ONI *follows her – she shimmies around* GILLIAN.

What is dis?

Baby wants ar party. Don't you baby?

ONI *circles – too close for comfort.*

Why can't we juss for one night be like normal teenagers /

You kill my vibe Gill-li-an you know dat?

Like really piss me off /

GILLIAN   You think you are like /

ONI   Like what? /

GILLIAN   Those girls that go out at night all dress up and high heels and have money to drink and call each other babes.

ONI   I can party babes!

GILLIAN   Where?

ONI   Champions. I have been to Champions /

GILLIAN   To ask for a cleaning job /

ONI   I stay dere for some time talk to owner and even
             have ar drink /

GILLIAN   Of orange juice.

ONI   Say what you like but you will never get into
             Champions. When you are older /

GILLIAN   We are the same age /

ONI   I have done more than you girlfriend /

GILLIAN   There is nothing special about Champions.

             I go to different places too. I go to see the girls in
             hairdresser the other day. They look so beautiful.
             Not too much make-up, wearing nice clothes. Not
             like girls in Champions /

ONI   Which hairdresser?

             Which hairdresser open in de night-time?

GILLIAN   –

ONI   Gill-li-an did you leave here in de day?

             Gilli-li-an? /

GILLIAN   They give me the picture. For you. I tell them
             about your skills Oni /

ONI   You tell dem about me?

GILLIAN   They were kind people. They want to talk about
             baby /

ONI   Why Gill-li-an?

             Beat.

GILLIAN   If I go to talk to doctor /

ONI   What doctor?

            We don't have doctor /

GILLIAN   They open in evening /

ONI   So?

GILLIAN   There is one nice woman there on the front of
            desk /

ONI   You went in? Have you nevar heard of CCTV?

GILLIAN   She say if I go to see doctor then maybe they help
            me. Help baby /

ONI   Ar you actually mad?

            Dey saw you?

            You let dem see you Gill-li-an?

GILLIAN   Just her. Just talking to her. She was so kind Oni
            and she was talking to me and telling me about
            how big baby is now. And how much baby wants
            to come out now. She have warm hands and /

ONI   You let har touch your belly? /

GILLIAN   She have warm hands and this smile like happy.
            She remind me of my grandmother the way she
            smile. Her hair. The way her hair be short and
            grey, she remind me of everything at home, and I
            let her touch my baby because /

ONI   Your baby? /

GILLIAN   She was telling me about baby club. To help
            young mothers. That's what she call me –

            Young mother like you.

            And swimming club for babies. She gives me
            leaflet and all the baby on there so cute.

            Woman at the desk say they can help us. They can
            get us a good place. Me and baby. She even tell
            me how they give me bag with all baby things like
            nappies, and books /

ONI   You have ar bag. I give dis good Ghana-must-go.
              It can carry anythin' /

GILLIAN   I want to…

              I want to make…

              Home for me and baby. Oni I want baby to be
              happy. I want to hold baby and kiss her and…

              I have no family now /

              GILLIAN is rocking back and forth in pain –

ONI   Go den!

              Go to dem. See if dey will look aftar you like me.

              Dere's de door…

              Do you want me to open it for you?

              *ONI marches towards the door – her hand hovers
              over the handle*

GILLIAN   –

ONI   Dey will force you to give your baby away.

              Dey will look at your belly. Dey will send to you
              back to Vietnam. That big dark bird will be
              looking you in de eyes and you will have no place
              to escape to den. Dere will be no Oni, no dancing,
              and no baby. Dey will give your baby to
              somebody else /

GILLIAN   Take my baby? /

ONI   Yes Gill-li-an.

              *GILLIAN scrambles in her bag until she finds the
              leaflet –*

              She hands it to ONI.

              Dey get you in dere. Den dey tell you all about
              how dey will look aftar baby. How dey will make
              you and baby better, but you know what dey do?
              I have told you over and over ageen Gill-li-an.

I have seen it. I have seen dem do it. Dey will take your baby. Den dey will take you to dat place…

ONI *tears the leaflet into tiny pieces –*

It is like you have forgotten everythin' I tell you Gill-li-an.

GILLIAN   You tell me too much /

ONI   You forget all de questions dey will ask you?

GILLIAN   No /

ONI   Tell me den /

GILLIAN   Oni! /

ONI   I don't believe you.

           Beat.

GILLIAN   When did you farst come?

           ONI *nods –*

ONI   Who brought you?

GILLIAN   How old are you?

ONI   What is your barth date?

GILLIAN   We don't believe you.

ONI   How old are you?

GILLIAN   Where are you living?

ONI   Do you know de word illegal? What about immigrant?

GILLIAN   Why are you here?

ONI   Are you making money?

           ONI *circles* GILLIAN –

And dey will look at you and your dirty dirty clothes and dose eyes touching your things. Even if you are crying hard, dey do not care…

It is all bad news girlfriend!

Beat.

It won't be long Gilli-li-an. Aftar today…

GILLIAN   I go for baby not for me.

Baby.

This baby.

Baby can't wait /

ONI   And what about me? So all dis time I am looking aftar you and baby, Gill-li-an juss thinking about Gill-li-an /

GILLIAN   Baby /

ONI   Gill-li-an you don't need doctor. You need me.

ONI *moves towards her –*

What is your name?

Short beat.

What. Is.Your. Name?

GILLIAN   Gillian /

ONI   Nice name. My name is Oni. O-Nee.

Can you pronounce?

It means born on holy ground.

Because I was born outside de church. My modder was praying in church one Sunday and den suddenly I want to come out. When she went outside to get some air, I juss dropped out dere on de ground. My fadder was dere and said it was like I came out running.

GILLIAN *lets a little smile slip –*

Is baby's fadder here?

GILLIAN   He is coming for us.

ONI   He is young like you?

GILLIAN   I am not a child /

ONI   What is de colour of his hair?

               Is he fit?

               I bet he have blue eyes…

GILLIAN   He have eyes that make you want to faint. When
               he look at you with those eyes…

               He will come for us. Me and baby.

               *ONI walks away and come back with two mugs –
               one has a broken handle.*

               She places a cup in front of GILLIAN, *and takes a
               seat.*

ONI   Drink it. I have put lots of sugar.

GILLIAN   I don't have money /

ONI   Don't worry about dat. Today I do two women's
               hair. Two. One aftar de odder. One girlfriend's har
               hair was like trying to plait peppercorn.

               Dey say me 'You're so much better den de
               hairdressers.' I say dem 'Oh good' but no tell
               anybody. Shsssh!

               ONI mockingly puts a finger to her lips –

               Dey think I am grown woman too. If they know I
               am juss seventeen den dey try to pay you less
               money.

               You want me to buy you cake?

               Beat.

               Why were you standing dere?

               Who are you running from?

               Vietnam yeah girlfriend?

Well you ar very lucky den dat you meet your
girlfriend Oni. Oni be de only girlfriend you need
on street.

ONI *does a kind of superhero pose* –

GILLIAN   I don't feel lucky Oni. You know the longest I have
been in the dark? I mean the longest time without
any light on my own? So dark. No lights. Darker
than this. Three days. It start that night when you
don't come back. When you leave here and go to
get you leave-to-remain paper, you are smiling and
dancing, and you tell me we will get somewhere to
live now. Proper house where you can do women's
hair in de day, go to college in evening and make
enough money to send back home to your mum.
You say after today your mother, your mum be
proud of you again. And I wait.

And I was waiting for you. Maybe she is plaiting
hair. Busy doing neat weave. Sewing the hair with
your needles and then doing the best lace front any
woman has ever had on her head. Making
someone somewhere look like her hair not from a
factory somewhere in India.

GILLIAN *attempts to kiss her teeth* –

She come back after hair I am thinking. She will
come back for her Gillian. And when darkness
come, I don't want to leave because maybe you
come back when I am out. So I bury myself. Use
everything I have in my bag and I bury myself in
them. Cover my whole head and face until I only
see dark. No light. And if the light tried to come
near me /

ONI   I came back / I am here now Gill-li-an –

GILLIAN   And I start to find food from bins behind Chinese
takeaway. For those days anything is better than
here.

ONI   But *here* is home /

GILLIAN   Home has a good bed and warm clothes /

ONI   What do you know about home?

I have ar home. I have ar home wiff green green leaves and streams and rivers. I have ar home wiff brodders and sisters. And dere I was nevar alone. I was nevar on my own. And now. Now if I go back, it will nevar be de same. My modder will nevar look at me de same way. I will nevar be able to run to har when I am crying. She will nevar believe in me ageen, and if I think of har looking at me like a stranger…

My own modder?

And dose streams and rivers will not be de same. Nothing will be de same. I will be alone. Dat I am sure of Gill-li-an. I will be alone.

GILLIAN   Why didn't you come back that night Oni? Why?

You promised?

ONI *turns to* GILLIAN –

ONI   I am here.

GILLIAN *lowers her head onto table and stares out* –

Gill-li-an?

GILLIAN   You are here?

ONI   Now.

Yes.

ONI *runs to stereo and turns on loud Afro-beat/dance music* –

GILLIAN*'s waters break* –

She stretches an arm out towards ONI.

ONI, *with her back to* GILLIAN, *continues dancing* –

Lights –

Scene Four

Four days after that day.

GILLIAN   Where is my baby? Is she still here? I hear her cry.

I hear her cry and I am sure she crying for me.

Can I see her?

You know what I call her?

You have to call her by her name.

Stop her crying. Make her happy.

Her name is Victoria Beatrice.

Me and Oni choose it.

Gillian…

My name is Chi Anh Nguyen.

A strip light comes on –

GILLIAN *holds her hands up to shield her eyes from the light –*

Beat.

Please don't turn the light on.

I can see you without the light.

Please.

You don't understand the darkness is where I can see everything.

I don't want you to look at me this way…

No not boyfriend. Not boy. He doesn't have blue eyes. He is not young like me. A man.

A man that Uncle know. My uncle who my father trust to look after his daughter. He trust Uncle. His best friend for so long.

My father who put his girl on a plane to UK. My
father trust Uncle to put me in study, look after
me. He did for first few months but then when
college ask for visa again in new term, he say he
can't find passport. Then he say he have to get
new passport. He doesn't care. Like he plan it. I
say I want to go home but now this time my uncle
start to say I have to do something for his friend.
He say his friend good man. Him and his wife
want baby but she is old, and so hard in UK to get
baby. He say they pay a lot. Enough for new
passport, and for me go back to study.

I have to stop school./The man come, and he come
every day for many weeks. He come to the house
all the time after work.

He try to be kind. He bring flowers and chocolate
and sometimes he stay to talk after.

He always bring test for baby. Then one day test
show two lines. He buy me takeaway food and
give Uncle a car.

I grow big. I am very sick. Every day eat and sick.
One day Uncle say man give him money to buy
me clothes to look nice so we go shopping in
centre with Uncle. I look in mirror and I can see it.
Bump. It is getting bigger. I want it. I don't know.
Maybe I don't want it…

I go to toilet and I see where you wash hands is
window. I see the window and start climbing. I run
so fast it feel like there is no ground. I don't see
where until I stop.

Beat.

And before I am speaking to my father all the time
on telephone. Uncle speak to him say visa coming
soon. Now I don't tell my daddy. I can't tell him.
My uncle tell him I leave my study and run away.
He tell him that I am bad girl. Have many
boyfriend.

How my father look at me now? Like prostitute?

Beat.

I want to be good for baby. I want to look after her now, Oni will help me.

Oni. Oni? My friend?

Me and my friend stay there together? She was there with me? She will tell you. She is a good person. Like my father...

Are you good person? Will you help me and baby?

The strip lights flicker down –

Lights down.

Scene Five

That day.

ONI *and* GILLIAN *are both lying on the floor on their backs. They have gathered candles around them.*

ONI   Imagine Gill-li-an.

Imagine Gill-li-an. Imagine anodder place ware we ar happy. Dis place will not have broken toilet or damp everyware. It will have curtains and someware for us to put our clothes. It will be ar proper house, on ar quiet, clean road, and we will have ar door dat we can open any time /

GILLIAN   Where will the house be? Which street?

ONI   Dere will be ar small table wiff flowers on it and ar big TV. We will have ar TV Gill-li-an. And ar kitchen. I will cook food and we won't have to eat from tin can. We will eat from plates every day.

GILLIAN   Which work we going to get? How will we pay
            for this Oni?

ONI   You will have ar room wiff ar bed, and pictures on
            de wall and it will be our place. Your blue-eyed
            boy can visit sometimes…

            And in it will be everythin' we can imagine. And
            when we look up to de sky…

            Your baby will see de sun. Feel it on har face.
            Your baby girl /

GILLIAN   Oh fuck!

ONI   Does it hurt bad de pain?

            GILLIAN *moves closer to* ONI –

GILLIAN   What time is it?

ONI   It is dat time after we went to sleep minus our
            naughty dreams plus de rest of our lives.

            Actually fourteen minutes past five. Dis baby has
            to come before it gets light /

            GILLIAN *gets to her feet – holds on to the wall to
            steady herself –*

ONI   Gill-li-an?

GILLIAN   I think I need the toilet.

            I really have to /

            GILLIAN *grunts louder and falls to her knees –*

            The baby is coming /

ONI   What? Are you sure?

GILLIAN   Oni!

            ONI *paces –*

            GILLIAN *is now groaning/screaming/hissing in
            some kind of a loop –*

ONI   I get you wata.

ONI *runs to the table and grabs a bottle of water –*

GILLIAN   I think I am going to die /

ONI   No. No.

            GILLIAN *screams louder –*

            What is your name?

GILLIAN   Gillian /

ONI   Nice name. My name is Oni. O-Nee.

            Can you pronounce?

            It means born on holy ground.

GILLIAN   Because you were born outside a church. You were born running /

            ONI *holds out the cup of water –*

ONI   Drink it.

            You want me to buy you cake /

GILLIAN   I like cake.

            I am really hungry now.

ONI   I am thinking maybe aftar we go to see what food dey throw arway. I think of spare rib all de time you know dat? If barbecue ribs ware ar man I would marry him /

GILLIAN   Why not just marry the pig?

ONI   Don't be silly. I can't marry ar pig. Eh eh if dey do dat one ware you come from I feel sorry for you /

GILLIAN   Fuck /

ONI   It was ar joke Gill-li-an.

GILLIAN   –

ONI   My fadder was dere and said it was like I come out running…

GILLIAN	He is not coming.
ONI	He is young like you?
GILLIAN	I am just a child Oni /
ONI	You are not meant to say it like dat! We will have to start ageen now.

What is your name?/

GILLIAN	Gillian /
ONI	Nice name. My name is Oni. O-Nee.

Can you pronounce?

It means born on holy ground.

GILLIAN *doubles over and grunts loudly –*

GILLIAN   I can see it is getting light. It is morning.

They will see me /

ONI   Okay close legs for ar minute girlfriend. Let me juss think how /

GILLIAN   We can't stop it now.

ONI   Dere is some things I have to tell you Gill-li-an.

I mean de thing is dis…

My family are de ones doing it most of de time so…

Like de women. Dey do it. I have not even watched one.

Barth.

What I mean is dat I am still learning Gilli-li-an.

What I mean is dat…

I no know anythin' about baby delivery!

ONI *walks towards the door – frozen in front of it.*

GILLIAN *sits knees up, panting from the pain –*

GILLIAN   I can't do this /

ONI   You can do dis Gill-li-an. You ar kind of
            superhero.

            Maybe baby fadder come too and maybe /

GILLIAN   He doesn't have blue eyes.

ONI   Someone will come for you /

GILLIAN   But we never trust them before /

ONI   Now is good time to start…

            The door opens –

            ONI *disappears in an instant –*

            Lights streams into the room –

            GILLIAN *is alone –*

GILLIAN   Oni where are you? Oni come back.

            GILLIAN*'s eyes search the room –*

            I think about all the nice lovely hair I am doing on
            baby. One week twist, one week cornrow, another
            week just like wavy extensions. The most
            beautiful one.

            GILLIAN *screams out –*

            Full house lights on.

Scene Six

The next day.

GILLIAN *in the Perspex box –*

GILLIAN   They try to buy my baby but I don't take the
             money. I don't take it. Oni will tell you. She make
             me brave. She stay with me. Look after me.
             She will look after baby too. She says my baby is
             special. Special baby girl. She is the best
             girlfriend.

             Oni. Oni? My friend? Me and my friend stay there
             together. She was there with me. Just before the
             light came in, she was there.

             The most special thing about her is her hair.
             All the way long to her waist. Shine like
             something out of shampoo advert. I watch her
             sometimes when she is sleeping next to me. And if
             you looked hard, really hard you could see lights
             in there. It was not just lights. It is like a whole
             galaxy of the smallest stars and each star has light
             so bright you can't look at it for too long.

             Oni is a special kind of girlfriend. Every
             girlfriends on the street know her. Ask them. She
             appear when you feel most lonely. When you are
             sleeping on cold ground, she comes and holds
             your hand. When you are scared, looking up to the
             sky waiting for that thing to find you, amongst the
             reeds, she whispers in your ear. And she says –

             – My name is Oni. O-Nee.

             Can you pronounce?

             It means born on holy ground.

             And she choose me. You ever have friend like
             that? Oni she know everything inside me. Like she
             is inside me. She is me. Everything about me.

GILLIAN *rummages in her coat pocket and pulls out a folded-up picture of a woman – typical of a Black-hair-salon ad –*

Can you see?

Short beat.

Have you seen my Oni? Where is she? You take her away? She was my friend.

Lights dim.

The End.

A Nick Hern Book

House + Amongst the Reeds first published in Great Britain in 2016 as a paperback original by Nick Hern Books Limited, The Glasshouse, 49a Goldhawk Road, London W12 8QP, in association with Clean Break

House copyright © 2016 Somalia Seaton
Amongst the Reeds copyright © 2016 Chino Odimba

The authors have asserted their moral rights

Cover image courtesy of Lorna Simpson and Salon 94, New York

Designed and typeset by Nick Hern Books, London
Printed in Great Britain by Mimeo Ltd, Huntingdon, Cambridgeshire PE29 6XX

A CIP catalogue record for this book is available from the British Library

ISBN   978 1 84842 613 9

www.nickhernbooks.co.uk

 facebook.com/nickhernbooks

 twitter.com/nickhernbooks